Lessons *from* *Leela*

*Sometimes you have to
let life live you...*

by

Lianne Campbell

Grosvenor House
Publishing Limited

This book is published by
Grosvenor House Publishing Ltd
28-30 High Street, Guildford, Surrey, GU1 3EL.
www.grosvenorhousepublishing.co.uk

A CIP record for this book
is available from the British Library

ISBN 978-1-78148-908-6

For Anousha;
may there always be the magic of 'Leela' in your life.

FOREWORD

I first heard the word 'Leela' when I was learning to play congas on a Brazilian Percussion course. Our teacher always emphasised feeling the music, feeling the drum, and letting the rhythm play you rather than trying to master it. One day, the group was struggling with a particularly tricky rhythm. As we thudded out the sounds and tried to grasp the counts and theory, our teacher's patience gave in to his fiery Brazilian spirit.

"No, stop, stop!" he shouted. "It is 'orrible, this noise! I want you to get into Leela when you play! Leela! You understand what is Leela?" He went on to explain that Leela was a Sanskrit word, loosely translated to mean 'divine dance of life', or 'miracle' and it was also used to describe the state musicians get into when they allow the music to play them; the state dancers go into when the dance dances them; when composers let the music be written; when writers let the book write them...

I recounted the incident to my partner, Josh, and Leela became our chosen name for the child we were longing to conceive, should it be a girl.

Years later, we handed over that heavenly name to our ten-week-old spaniel; not quite what we had imagined in our ideal baby-naming ceremony but hey, life can be like that. Sometimes you just have to let life live you...

Chapter One

THE END

July 2008

The door to Flat 4, Kilgannon House slammed shut for the very last time. I stared at the brown wood with its familiar grainy pattern and resisted the urge to dive into my pocket, fumble for the key and open it again. It was too late. The moment was gone and there was no point in trying to relive it. I had wanted a ceremonious exit over the threshold, a conscious step into the big wide world. Instead, we had bundled clumsily over it with the last of our possessions, all elbows and baggage, leaving the door to swing itself shut with a callous bang.

I felt a lump rise in my throat and at that moment, Rick, our about to be ex-neighbour, opened his door to see us on our way. I bit my lip and willed myself not to cry; *not now, please not now, not in front of Rick*. Not that it would have mattered. Rick was as sad as we were that we would no longer be neighbours. It was just that I wanted this to be a happy occasion. I wanted to show the world how excited I was. After all, everything was fine, this was the beginning of our great adventure. Our home was now the van and it was the start of something brilliant. We had finally thrown caution to the wind and our hearts over the bar. Only at this moment I was starting to wish we'd thrown them on a boomerang.

Leela sat close and was unusually still and quiet, not taking her eyes off me for a second. I knew she was looking for reassurance and, as top dog, it was my job to do that; to let her know that she was safe, I knew what I was doing and would take good care of her. I smiled weakly at her. Unconvinced, her eyes widened even more. Remembering the language of the Dog Listener, I took a deep breath, broke eye contact to assume confidence, stood up straight and placed a clear thought in my head that all was well. Nervously, she moved closer to my leg. Damn it, dogs always know what you're feeling.

Leela had been sick in the last hour of us being in the flat. Her tail that normally wagged continuously from morning 'til night had been strangely still. She had followed us everywhere as we put the last of our stuff into bags and did the final bits of cleaning. It had been an emotional day; in fact, it had been an emotional five weeks. I had gone from exhilarated to petrified, with not much respite in between. I must have been a joy to live with! Despite the emotional roller coaster, though, everything felt right, since we had been asking for a push from the universe and an adventure from life. Life being life, though, it came in a package we weren't expecting at all and, as with all true stories, how it all started goes back a long way. But more of that later.

We had spent the past few hours saying goodbye and preparing our old home for the new tenants. Josh, who had been steady as ever in the last weeks, was now as emotional as me. He'd been fine until our friend Russell phoned to see how we were getting on. I had picked up the phone with a cheery "Hello" and heard Russell say, "How's it going?"

My breath caught in my throat. I pinched myself hard, smiled into the phone, got the words, "Great! Fantastic! We're really excited" ready in my mouth... and then burst into tears. "It's all empty and bare and ... and ... and ... it's empty and bare and empty!" I cursed the affirmation I'd chanted religiously for the last month: "I express myself clearly when under pressure."

Russell, known by Josh and myself as Russell Big-heart, was living up to his name and pouring words of wisdom and reassurance in my ear but I couldn't hear anything he was saying. I was staring at the beautiful, sunshine-yellow walls of our gorgeous home as the last rays of July sun shone through the huge ceiling-to-floor windows that looked out directly onto the sea. There was a magical glow all around the room. God, this place was special. I numbly handed the phone to Josh and was taken aback when I saw he had huge tears in his eyes. So it wasn't just me being over-dramatic, this really was hard. This had been our home for nearly ten years and the only place either of us had settled in since leaving the homes we had grown up in. It had also been the home I had moved into just before we had met and it had soon become 'ours', which had been a big commitment for both of us.

Josh mumbled a quick end to the conversation with Russell and put the phone down. We stood in the middle of the room and held each other. Leela pushed herself in between our feet, which made us cry and laugh at the same time. She was the catalyst for all of this. In the eight amazing months she had been part of our lives, she had wreaked glorious havoc and we had no desire to turn back time and change anything, not one thing. She had entered our world and hit centre in a way neither of us had expected, certainly not Josh, who wasn't a doggy person at all. Now we were a family, the three musketeers, the explorers, the pioneers of our own future the bravest of the...

"Let's go." Josh's voice jarred me back into the room and I realised he had moved on from the moment whilst I had dropped to my knees and was sobbing into the ears of a rather alarmed-looking spaniel. I needed to get a grip! I stood up and prepared myself to go.

I once read a book by Karen Kingston who specialises in Feng Shui and space clearing, in which she explained how she would enter a building and stroke the walls in order to make a connection and encourage it to tell its story. I decided that would be a good way to say my last goodbye to our dear flat, which I had christened 'Sunshine'. I stroked the living room wall and said thank you. I began to feel overwhelming amounts of love and appreciation. Everything seemed to be moving in slow motion, my heart filled with gratitude and I was aware of every detail of the wall, the way the light fell on it, the coolness and texture under my hand. I became totally immersed in this precious moment.

And then the memories began to flood in. The cosy nights and days watching the wild sea as the rain lashed against the window; sunbathing in the living room with the windows flung open; gatherings and parties with friends, visits from our families; romantic moments after a day on the beach; glasses of wine watching the sun going down. I willed all the memories the walls held to flood back into me one more time.

Then a more recent one popped in. My sister Kaye had phoned up the week before, saying, "Put Channel 4 on now, there's a programme about people who fall in love with buildings. Weird." The phone went dead and I knew she was probably phoning my other sister to repeat the same instruction as I crossed the room to put the TV on. We would have one of those "Oh my God, can you believe it?!" conversations at a later date.

She was right, it was weird. The last ten minutes showed a woman fulfilling her dream as she sat straddling the Eiffel Tower with no underwear on. Thankfully, she did have her over-garments on but that still left little else to the imagination as she shared her triumph with the nation.

"Weird." My sister's voice echoed in my head and I froze mid-stroke and moved away from the wall. Suddenly very self-conscious and acutely aware that my bizarre behaviour was being witnessed, I turned my head around slowly and met Josh's bewildered gaze. My eyes dropped downwards to Leela, who wore the same expression. Time to swiftly move on! I cleared my throat and said loudly, with all the dignity I could muster, "Okay, flat, thanks for a lovely time," then added a cheerful, "Look after the next tenants as much as you looked after us." Then we all turned our backs on the living room, marched down the hallway and shuffled ourselves, and the last of our possessions through the front door. It slammed shut.

So here we were on the other side at the beginning of a new chapter. We had arranged for Rick to take our Dyson while we were on the road. We had shared it whilst we were neighbours and often enjoyed enthusing over its efficiency as we passed it back and forth between the two flats. I watched Josh hand it over now and everything seemed to go in slow-motion again. I loved that hoover! Oh this was ridiculous, what did I mean I loved that hoover? What a stupid thought. I hate hoovering, I do anything to get out of it. But as I looked at our beautiful Dyson, I wanted to snatch it back, open Flat 4 again and lovingly vacuum its beautiful floors to make up for all the times I had resented it.

"Weird." The memory of my sister's voice jolted me back. I pulled my gaze away from the household appliance I was aching for and smiled shakily at Rick.

"Well, look after yourself," I managed to squeak. I could taste blood on my lip where I had bitten it so hard. Rick hugged me, and Charlie, his thirteen-year-old son, appeared at his side. I forgot about the Dyson and felt sad to be leaving the humans who stood in front of me and relieved to be having normal feelings again. We would miss them – not that we had lived in each other's pockets, or even been in each other's flats that much, for that matter, but we had been good neighbours and we did watch out for each other.

"Where will home be tonight then?" asked Rick.

We hadn't fully decided. We actually only had one night before Josh was to go on a course in Dorset whilst Leela and I stayed with my friend Sally for a few days on the other side of Brighton. We had considered the seafront, and Stanmer Park where a lot of other travellers parked up but, although it was already 8.30pm and we were hungry and tired, we were both feeling it would be more adventurous to go out of Brighton for the first night.

Rick suggested *The Anchor* in Barcombe. "If you eat there, they'll probably let you stay in the car park for the night." That sounded like a great idea. Barcombe was about half an hour's drive away. We knew the Anchor and the thought of a good meal and a drink appealed to us both.

We said our goodbyes and went down the stairs, out of the building and across the road into our new home, Romany, a Peugeot boxer camper van. We climbed in and Leela wagged her tail, seeming relieved to be out of the intensity of the flat. The van was a state. The plan had been to have everything in its place by the time we left. However, despite our good intentions, it hadn't quite worked out. Packing up and getting the stuff we wouldn't need into storage, had taken much longer than we expected. We had already extended our stay in the flat by a week and, in the end, we just shoved everything willy-nilly into the van to be sorted out later. Only now was later and our new home looked like we had loaded up for a trip to the tip! Every bit of space was taken up with clothes, plates, cups, dog towels, food, shoes, raincoats etc, etc.

We climbed into the front, Josh in the driving seat and me in the passenger seat, with Leela on my knee. We looked across at each other and smiled. Leela yawned and snuggled her head under my arm, obviously feeling secure again. In fact, we all felt secure again; relieved and happy that the worst was over, we had left the flat and it felt good to be on this side of the story. We had finally stepped into our future.

Josh touched the picture of Ganesh, remover of all obstacles, that sat on the dashboard. This is his usual ritual at the start of a journey and one of the things I love about his Indian culture. Then he beckoned fate by starting the engine. Our new life had begun.

Chapter Two

IT'S NOT WHERE
YOU START...

We swung the van out of Norfolk Square and headed out of town. We decided to ignore the mess in the van for tonight as we wanted to celebrate, have a drink, a good meal and sleep in a pretty village in the countryside; the perfect first night. This was the life! I pulled Leela closer to me and felt happy. I was with the two beings I loved most in the world and about to experience a whole different way of living. The sun was starting to go down and a red glow was cast on the country lanes. I loved the feeling of the weight of Leela's warm body as she leaned against me and slept in my arms. I glanced over at Josh. He looked beautiful as he drove along, a glint of anticipation in his big brown eyes. I would remember this moment forever. I felt free and content. It couldn't get any better than this.

We pulled up in the car park of the Anchor. It was empty. There was nobody in the garden and no lights on in the pub.

"It's closed," Josh said.

Wanting to keep the optimism going, I said, "Let's go and see. It may just be quiet, maybe we can just have a bar snack and a quick drink."

We parked the van, and walked over to the pub. Sure enough, it was well and truly shut. It was also getting late and we didn't fancy driving around looking for somewhere else to stay. After a few minutes of looking at the closed door with gormless expressions, we decided to stay in the car park anyway, as that way we could get an early night and wake up feeling refreshed.

Leela was exploring. I looked around to call her to me and spotted her in the corner of the garden, flat on her back, having the time of her life gleefully wallowing in a big pile of fox poo! Now, if you have had the good fortune never to have been in contact with a dog that has rolled in fox poo, you may not fully appreciate why van + dog + fox poo + humans do not make up the recipe for a great night in.

I shooed her off it and clipped her lead on but it was too late, she stank. We had no way of washing her as we hadn't filled the water tank up yet and the only place for her to sleep was with us on the bed. Great. It was then we noticed that there was a light on in the pub upstairs. The people who lived there were obviously in, so we went back to the van quickly, to spend the rest of the evening in the dark in order to avoid drawing attention to ourselves, as the last thing we needed was to be moved on in the middle of the night.

We moved the piles of stuff off the bed and loaded it all on to the front seats. We were hungry, but the kitchen was out of bounds as we couldn't get to the cupboards. Josh found a large packet of crisps on top of a basket of cutlery. We sat in the dark and shared them, with Leela, stinking, in the middle of us. It started to rain.

"We'll get used to this," I said nervously.

"It's just a case of feeling more confident about just pulling up and sleeping wherever we are," said Josh. "We've done it enough when we've travelled, it's no different living permanently in a van. We'll be okay. Just remember, we know that this was the right move."

I don't think either of us felt that reassured as we climbed into bed that night and we both knew we were putting a brave face on for each other. We cuddled up close, and Leela wandered up the middle to snuggle up, oblivious to the foul smell she was subjecting us to. I closed my eyes tight and prayed things would take an up-turn in the morning. At least it had stopped raining.

I woke up to the sound of light rain on the tin roof, which made me feel cosy. I squinted my eyes open in the direction of the little ledge where Josh kept his watch. It was 5.30am. I snuggled up to Josh. He was lovely and warm. Leela was curled around my feet at the bottom of the bed. I drifted back to sleep with the gentle pitter-patter of rain in my ears.

When I woke again a little later, it was raining harder. I wondered if it had been continuous through the night. The last few days had been gloriously warm and sunny but, with the great British summer, who knew whether that was summer done and dusted? I snuggled further down under the duvet. I didn't want to look around the van as I knew it resembled Primark in the mid-January sales. When the rain stopped, we would find a dry place and empty everything out. Put it all back nice and neatly and turn Romany into a little kingdom to be proud of. I spent the next hour drifting in and out of sleep, making plans to the soundtrack of rain beating hard against the van.

At 8.00, we decided the rain wasn't going to stop and we may as well get up and drive to Stanmer Park. There, Leela could bomb around to her heart's content and we could spend the morning sorting out the van before Josh dropped us off at Sally's and went to attend his course

At Stanmer Park, we threw everything off the front seats and onto the bed. We must have got used to the stink of fox poo as we couldn't smell it any more. I wasn't sure that it was a great thing to acclimatize your olfactory senses to, but I guess at this point in time it was more practical to be oblivious than house-proud.

The morning was challenging, to say the least. The rain was relentless and we had nowhere to keep our stuff dry other than inside the van, which was getting wetter by the minute as we had to leave a door open so we could keep an eye on Leela. We tried our best to get organised while Leela ran around in the mud and rain and thoroughly enjoyed herself. Every now and again, she would bomb into the open side door, eager to share her joy, only to be greeted by one of us screaming, "OUT!" She would shoot out again, equally as happy, tail wagging in anticipation of finding a new puddle to play in. Meanwhile, we frowned, huffed, puffed, sighed and struggled around each other and our possessions, trying to create a bit of order.

Leela had it right; come rain or shine, she was happy. She never woke up in a bad mood or was grumpy for no reason. Life was to be enjoyed. Rain was rain, wet was wet, muddy was muddy and smelly was smelly. Pure acceptance. Wherever she was and whatever the circumstance, she always chose to throw herself into every day with gusto. I envied her. She often broke my mood when I felt stressed or unhappy. I'd be in mid frown, thinking about an issue with work, or grumbling about the weather and she would trot in, drop a ball in front of me and do her funny backward walk to entice me to play, reminding me that there were much better and more important things to focus on in life. Like enjoying yourself.

This morning, though, she just couldn't snap me out of it. I was wet and cold and not looking forward to saying goodbye to Josh. The thought of leaving him to go off in our home made me feel uprooted and insecure. I was surprising myself. I had spent fourteen years of my life as a professional dancer, travelling the world with everything I owned in a suitcase and I had loved it. When I was in my twenties and early thirties, I house-shared or stayed in hotels, B&Bs or caravans. In between contracts, I stayed with friends or went back home to Manchester to see my family.

I had always thought of myself as a free spirit, yet here I was, at forty-three, realising that I had got into some very staid habits in the last ten years. I was more settled now, and even though Josh and I still travelled a lot with our work, in the last ten years we had always had the flat to come back to. Our stuff was always there. It was home and my heart had felt settled. Did that mean it wasn't free any more? Or was I just having yet another mood swing? I wasn't sure.

By eleven, we had created some sort of order and I called Sally and told her to prepare for a filthy dog to be thrown in her shower. We headed back into Brighton with Leela, who was firmly instructed to sit still in the well of the passenger seat. Apart from a few spontaneous shudders of joy, she did pretty well. I smiled weakly at her attempts to engage me in her merriment and comforted myself with the idea that damp splatters of mud on one's face gave one a look of a wild, mystic traveller!

Chapter Three

TEA AND CAKE

Sally lived in a terraced house in the Hanover area of Brighton; a popular area with cars parked either side of the narrow roads, not leaving much time to stop before being hooted at. As we approached the house, I pecked Josh on the cheek, grabbed Leela's lead in one hand and my bag in the other and tumbled out of the van as quickly as possible, with a "See you in a few days, have a great course."

He looked a bit startled at my abrupt exit, but I was determined to get my spirits up before I went into Sally's house. I was annoyed with myself for feeling so miserable, having not yet lived in the van for twenty-four hours. What was the matter with me? Where had my adventurous spirit gone? Happiness was a choice, right? As I walked up Sally's driveway, I took a few deep breaths and ran through all the things I was grateful for in my life – or, at least, as many as I could get through in the few seconds I had before the door opened.

"Hello! Hello, Leela pup." Sally's bright, pretty face smiling warmly at us was suddenly added to my list of things to be grateful for.

"Hiya, out of the way, one smelly puppy coming through!" I bustled in cheerily, threw my bags down, picked Leela up and ran up the stairs to the bathroom before anyone could get a whiff or a proper look at the state of her. Not that it mattered to Sally, she loved Leela to bits. Her beautiful Gordon Setter Cross, Digby, had died recently at the grand old age of thirteen. He was a lovely character; if he had been human, he would have been a surfer dude, laidback, easy-going and aware of his charm. Digby had always enjoyed the company of the ladies and would lounge around, expecting to be drooled over. He was rarely disappointed. Understandably, Sally missed him terribly and a burst of doggy energy in her life was always welcome.

As I showered Leela, I continued with my thoughts of gratitude, focusing on the feel of her little wet body as I washed her in the warm water and enjoying lathering the stubborn, sticky fox poo out of her coat and watching the mud drop off. She looked at me, stiff-bodied and still-tailed, letting me know that she didn't approve of bathing. I spoke softly to her and worked as quickly as I could. Every now and again, her eyes would begin to close as she gave in to the warm sensation of the water and rhythmic movements of the massage. I could never make up my mind whether she found it unpleasant or not, with these mixed messages. My sister's dogs responded in the same way, as did Scamp, the cocker spaniel we had when we were growing up.

I decided that they did enjoy it but protested on principle. A unanimous decision in the dog world to stand against bathing for dogs! After all, dogs were supposed to be out there jumping into rivers, running after balls, rolling in dirt and creating havoc. Not poncing themselves up with shampoo and making themselves smell nice. If they wanted to smell like shampoo, they'd roll in it! It was undignified for a dog to be scrubbed clean and important that they should stand together in protest.

I fantasised about the guidelines in the dog union rulebook.

Rule number 7: When bathing: Do not co-operate. Make it clear to your owner you do not and will not approve of this humiliating ritual invented for humans by humans.
Rules of conduct: Stand as stiff as you can and stare uncompromisingly at the nearest escape. Fix your head and do not allow it to be moved around so you can be shampooed easily on both sides. Do not, under any circumstances, obey commands to sit or lift your paws. Should your owner have to take their attention off you for a second for any reason, e.g. to take the cap off the shampoo or prepare the towel, shake wildly and pebbledash the bathroom tiles as much as possible with the bits of soap and mud you have managed to keep hidden under your ears and underbelly. If your owner cowers away from the offensive material, do not allow yourself feelings of sympathy; instead, make a bolt for the door.

"There we go," I cooed, "all clean now, wasn't too bad, was it?" She didn't answer. I reached over for the towel (one hand firmly on the back of her neck!). As I lifted her from the bath I could have sworn she muttered something under her breath.

I towel-dried her as much as possible and then cleaned out the bath as she ran round in circles in the tiny bathroom, ridding her body of any residual stress. As I opened the door, she threw herself out of it and shot downstairs, running and shaking at the same time, not wanting to be held back another moment from greeting whoever she may find in the kitchen. I love the way dogs always presume they are welcome wherever they are. Leela ran around Sally, her whole body writhing with pleasure at being able to grace her with her presence.

It felt nice and cosy in the kitchen. The rain was still beating hard against the French windows, the kitchen was warm, cake was on the table and the kettle was on. It felt good to be with a friend and I felt selfish about leaving Josh in such a rush. It would have been a wrench for him having me and Leela rush off like that, leaving him to drive off alone in the rain in our not-quite-organised-enough home.

"So how's it going so far?" Sally asked, handing me a piece of juicy-looking carrot cake and a steaming cup of tea. She let me babble at high speed for a while as I recalled the events of yesterday and what I had felt. As I talked, I felt my body relaxing and heard my voice slow down and lower an octave. I was in good company. She was a good friend, always ready to listen and encourage. I felt safe again with the decisions I had made and the situation I was in.

I met Sally when she became a member of the Samba band that I had joined the year before. Playing samba had opened up a completely new lease of life for me, as music was an area that I had always felt was 'out of bounds': a belief I formed after some negative comments at school and a traumatic experience involving a recorder and an insensitive teacher, when I was the tender age of eight. Joining a band was a big step all those years later and, although my progress was slow and I never quite got over the feeling I was out of my depth, I really enjoyed playing all the different instruments samba had to offer.

One of the hardest things about leaving Brighton was that I would have to leave the band. It had evolved from general samba into a particular style from the North of Brazil known as Maracatu; a style that had really captured my heart as it is incredibly exciting and hypnotic. We had a gig coming up at a festival the next month, which would be my last. My intention was to go out with a bang (excuse the pun), throw myself into the gig and see it as a completion of letting go of the incident that had led me to believe that I had no place in the world of creating music.

Chapter Four

SEEDS ARE PLANTED

I was reasonably bright and happy in my reception year at school, however, for reasons I can't quite remember, I was terrified of my Year One teacher. Not long after I started her class, I became introverted and nervous. More and more, I chose to play with my 'imaginary' friends rather than be with real people and I began to dread leaving the house. I would get a really high temperature just before we left for school in the morning and it would be back to normal within ten minutes of Mum saying I could stay home. I talked less and less and refused to go out and play with the other kids on our street, or go to anyone else's house. Mum tried her best to find out what was the matter but I would just go silent whenever she asked. Although I don't remember any details, only the feeling of being frozen and unable to communicate, I don't honestly think there was a particular traumatic event that occurred. It was more a drip-feed of gradual and persistent unease about being around a very strict teacher who wasn't very sensitive to how her manner affected others. I remember very little from that year at school, only her shouting a lot and also kidding us all, on one of her good days, that she was a witch and could cast spells on us. I think I just took her at her word and it had a big impact on me. I also remember her dragging one of the boys in my class down the dinner hall one lunchtime because he had been rude to her and refused to eat his dinner. It was around this time my breathing often felt tight and I seemed to always have a cold.

My social behaviour gradually improved once I moved on through the school, but I always had health niggles. By age eight I was diagnosed as mildly asthmatic and given inhalers and was still suffering persistent colds. Not being bright or particularly sporty, coupled with being painfully shy and rather plain-looking, didn't put me in the running for Student of the Year award.

In Year Four, I finally found something I loved to do at school, recorder lessons. I could never get my head around reading music, instead, I would listen a few times, pretend I was reading my music book and play along with everyone else. It worked a treat for me and it was good to have a time at school where I could escape. I found it for a while in music.

It was also good to have something to aspire to, and mine was to be a member of the school recorder group. The recorder group were all clever and popular and looked incredibly glamorous as they sat facing us at the front of the school assembly every morning. They played when we sang hymns and to me, they were perfect, they had it all. I would lie awake at night dreaming of the day I would be up there with the best of them, giving it large on the treble recorder and earning my status as most popular girl in the school. In fact, in my own little dream world, not only was I the most popular, I was also the cleverest and the prettiest girl in the school. I began to look forward to bedtime almost as much as I looked forward to recorder classes.

Unfortunately for me, the day came when my teacher decided she had had enough of my lying, faking ways. I was fully immersed in the beauty of hearing *Row, Row, Row Your Boat* tumble effortlessly out of my recorder when I realised that the rest of the class had gone quiet and our teacher, Mrs Fat Bottom Bossy Pants (I refuse to call her anything else since that awful day), was standing directly in front of my music stand.

Lips still clamped around my recorder, my eyes turned upwards to take in her huge, monster-like frame. She glared at me and then, with a nasty glint in her eye, she turned the page of my music book.

"Play that!" she hissed and I swear her tongue was forked and fire came out of her nostrils.

I bit my recorder hard and dragged my eyes away from her enormous face. I stared at the music on the page and it all went fuzzy, the dots danced around in front of my eyes and the lines started laughing at me. I looked up at the title in the desperate hope I would recognise it and be able to play the tune, but even if I knew the piece she was asking me to play, fear had my dyslexia firmly in its wicked hold. All the letters were jumbled.

"Well?" Her voice sounded like we were underwater. My face burned with shame, I froze and felt hot tears stinging my eyes. Mrs Fat Bottom Bossy Pants snatched my book off the stand and, marching back to her desk, announced to the class that "LIANNE" (I remember my name booming out the loudest), "still can't read music and…"

I didn't hear the rest. It was something about me being a waste of time, but it went in deep. I stared at the floor and thought I would die of shame, feeling so stupid to think I could fake it. Words are powerful. They can change your beliefs or how you feel about yourself, or anything else for that matter, in a second, leaving you spellbound for years. It was that point I decided it wasn't my place to play music if I couldn't do it properly and recorder lessons became something I did because I had to. Just like all the other stuff at school.

So life was looking a bit grim at age eight, with all my dreams shattered. Mum recognised that her middle child was slowly declining in all areas of her development and kept watching out for any remote signs of talent she could tease out of me. I would take a photo on a family holiday that would come out in focus and she would buy me a cheap camera and photography book for Christmas. I once showed an interest in how we digested food and I got a kid's microscope for my birthday.

Dance classes were one of her ideas, after noticing that I loved musicals and finding me pretending to tap dance on the kitchen floor. I came home from school one day and she announced she had booked me in for ballet and tap classes. I was furious with her. I think my shyness and dread of school had reached a point that anything to do with learning or meeting strangers terrified me. I burst into a tantrum and refused to go. Mum lost it with me at that point. At her wits' end and no doubt concerned for the future of my sanity, she dragged me, kicking and screaming, to the class on the Friday.

It was held in the local church hall and I arrived to see all the girls in pretty pink leotards with matching hair bands and dainty little ballet slippers. Like most eight -year-old girls, I liked how they looked, but I didn't like the fact that I was there by force and I was determined not to show any enthusiasm. I sulked and hid behind Mum as she introduced me to the teacher. Her name was Miss Coakley and she stood very straight and looked incredibly glamorous in her crimplene trousers and high-heeled mules. She smiled warmly at me and I scowled back. I avoided all eye contact with the other girls. In my P.E. shorts, t-shirt and socks, I felt self-conscious, to say the least.

When it was time for the class to begin, the pretty little delicate girls fluttered into the hall and I shuffled behind them, feeling like a footballer. I was probably no bigger than any of them, but ever since my recorder trauma, whenever I became self-conscious I felt like Alice in Wonderland after she had eaten the grow pill.

We started with bar work, which meant we all had to pull a chair into the middle of the room and hold onto the back of it. I made sure I got right to the back. Mum stayed with me, sitting at the back of the class and beaming support whenever she caught my eye. Thinking about it now, it must have been incredibly painful for her to see me in this situation. She knew how much I was suffering and must have been praying to all the gods of every religion that she had made the right decision in forcing me to come. She didn't know about the recorder incident. I never told a soul. I had just assumed that the teacher was right and my shame was justified. Mum just knew that I was unhappy and she wanted me to find something that would boost my confidence.

Mrs Beaty, who looked about a hundred and seven, shuffled up to the piano, fumbled for her glasses and began to play. A gentle classical melody filled the room.

"Just follow the other girls, Lianne," Miss Coakley's voice sang over the top of the music. It sounded kind. I felt scared. I just knew I was about to disappoint her and my mum.

I fixed my eyes on the girl in front and just copied everything she did. I was concentrating so hard that when I heard Miss Coakley say, "Lovely, Lianne, lovely," I thought, *did she really just say that? Do I really look lovely?* I felt myself fill with pride, my body relaxed and I began to enjoy myself. I was good at something at last.

Mum praised me all the way home and recounted the whole class to Dad and Nan when we got back, telling them how good I was. In actual fact, Mum had just spent the longest hour of her life watching her clumsy daughter bumble her way through a ballet class and praying the teacher would be kind enough to encourage her and give her some hope. Whether Miss Coakley had truly meant it, or whether she just wanted another child to enrol for a term in her dance school, didn't matter to Mum; she had seen me show signs of enjoying something at last.

That night, I went to bed bursting with joy and lay awake dreaming of being the most famous and, of course, the cleverest and prettiest, ballerina in the world.

Chapter Five

A CAREER PATH IS CARVED

Dance soon became the 'thing' I did. It felt so good to be part of something. In my weekly dance classes of ballet and tap, I learnt the set exercises, and I remember the thrill of moving in unison with the other girls. It was also something I could talk about. I felt I had an identity after feeling so invisible and insignificant in a culture that needs to find a purpose for everybody, even the very young. I was now 'A Dancer'.

Along with the praise and acceptance came a need to prove myself and along with that came a fear that I would be 'found out'. It's a funny thing, praise; the more we receive it, the more the outside world becomes the authority and it begins to speak louder than our own intrinsic reward of self approval that is so important for our feelings of safety and high self-esteem. More often than not, formal training only focuses on striving to be better. Doing something purely for the pleasure of it can easily get lost to this. Like many children, my relationship of dependence on acceptance and looking to the outside world for validation was strengthened, as the comments and structures put in place by well-meaning adults replaced the natural confidence we are all born with. Children know when praise is genuine. I felt some of it was, and I also knew that a lot of it was said in order to 'boost my confidence'. I wasn't 'a natural' and I went to great lengths to hide it. I wanted to have a special gift and I wanted to meet the expectations of others. So, I worked at getting good out of sheer determination to hang onto my identity.

When I danced in the privacy of my bedroom, I felt a release, a feeling of freedom, something I only used to glimpse in class as, over the years, it became more and more of a thing to be mastered, something you only showed once it had been perfected.

And so started my complex relationship with this beautiful art, that brought so much meaning and joy to my life. I loved being part of the shows, rehearsing with my newfound friends and I adored the sheer excitement of performing. Dance, like a jealous lover, was constantly seeking my attention, luring me into her magic, grace and tender touch and then confusing me with insecurities and put-downs that didn't need to belong to me, but which I accepted wholeheartedly. But I was smitten and had made up my mind that this was what I wanted to do, once I was free to take charge of my own life.

I can clearly remember the confused look on the face of the careers officer who came to our school to advise us all when I was in year eleven. The secondary school I went to wasn't exactly known for contributing to the cream of society. And, after choosing to settle into the roll of 'I'm dumb and don't care and just wanna have fun', I didn't do much in my years of secondary school to nudge the school's reputation higher up the ladder of respectability. Nobody moved house in order to ensure their child got into my school; in fact, as the years went on, more and more people in the private houses in the surrounding areas moved out! Today, where my school once shabbily stood, there is a small complex of spanking new, identical, tidy and clean Barrat houses with carpet-like mowed lawns and neat little window boxes, nestled in the middle of the two council estates that once surrounded our school. A symbol of how we prefer to remove the failures in our society and replace them with something more respectable, instead of giving them the support they so badly need.

My appointment with the careers officer was located in the damp storeroom that had been delegated the careers office for that day. Miss Norton gave me a tired smile and offered me a seat. On the desk in front of her lay me, summed up on a sheet of paper.

"So, Lianne, how can I help you today?"

Then, without looking at me, she placed my assessment aside and proceeded to direct me to a selection of 'opportunities' that fitted my abilities, none of which were of any interest to me or memorable enough to write about.

"Erm, thanks, but I know what I am doing," I said awkwardly. "I am going to be a dancer."

It was the first time I had made that declaration at school – "I am going to be a dancer" – and it felt weird. Dancing was wussy stuff at my school and I went to great lengths to hide the fact that I spent many of my evenings rehearsing or doing classes. A few people at school knew I went to dancing lessons, but I played it so low key that nobody seemed to pick up on it.

"Well, in order to do that, you would have to have had formal dance training," Miss Norton said authoritatively, with a hint of annoyance in her voice; she picked up my assessment and quickly scanned it for evidence.

"I do go to dance classes and I am going to be a dancer," I told her with even less conviction, and then fell silent as she looked at me with a mixture of confusion and irritation.

There was a long pause and then she blurted out in a confident tone, "You know it is an extremely difficult career path and I thoroughly advise you to have something to fall back on."

I checked out at this point and gazed unseeingly at the forms she put in front of me, letting her jabber on for fifteen minutes or so without listening, until it was time to leave the room.

Once I had said it out loud, and at school, and in the careers office, I somehow found it easy to say it when the subject came up with my peers. I only had four months to go before I could burn my uniform and set off for pastures new, so I didn't care any more. And, contrary to all my fears, none of my peers seemed to care what I was going to do, either. There were a few surprised looks and blank expressions, but my ambitions didn't seem to rock anybody's world. So much for my slinking about in secret all those years!

My dream of becoming a dancer was so strong; it was all I could think of. Even with the warnings from well-meaning adults (none of whom had the slightest bit of experience in my chosen profession), telling me that it was a difficult life, jobs were few and far between and competition was fierce, I still wouldn't be swayed. I knew what I was going to do and there was a girl at my dancing school who had already done it.

She was about four years older than me, and several grades ahead at dancing school. When she was eighteen, she had gone to dance with a company in Portugal. She was also my cousin's cousin so I used to hear news of her from time to time. I was so in awe of her that I would blush at the very mention of her name. She actually turned up at my cousin's house one day when I was also there and I was so disabled with shyness, I ran upstairs and sat on the toilet for her entire visit, praying she wouldn't need the loo. I was afraid I would faint with the enormity of coming face to face with this glamorous girl who was living my dream life. Where I was brought up, people didn't really do what Jackie had done. The done thing was to get a trade behind you and be grateful for a steady job. When Jackie Stevens went to dance in a Casino in Portugal, it seemed to me that that was all anyone talked about. She had made it! She was on the stage! I was determined to follow suit; I wanted to be exciting and talked about, too.

From the moment I left school, life took an upward swing. I was still in the final years of my ballet and tap exams. Once I had them, I would be qualified to teach. I wanted to do that before I set off on my wonderful dancing career, as that was the only thing I was willing to have to 'fall back on'. I had left school with a Grade 4 CSE in cooking and an equally low grade in English and sewing. I flunked the rest of my exams. I had been told in Primary School that the chances of me having any kind of academic success was probably nil and I dutifully fulfilled the prediction. The prospect of a job was pretty bleak so, yet again, my mum came to the rescue by dragging me along to a college open day, no doubt praying that this time I would finally find something more realistic to be interested in and change my mind about treading the boards. When I got there, I was delighted to find new subjects that sparked my interest and by the end of the day, I had signed up to do psychology, sociology, theatre studies and drama.

I loved college. I felt free; nobody forced me to do anything. It was great that there was no authority checking up on whether I had done my homework, telling me what to wear… in fact, there was nobody even checking whether I turned up for lessons. As a result, I dived into studying, partying and all the wonder and excitement of student life. I ended up staying on an extra two years to do A-levels in my much-loved subjects. In short, I found what twelve years of school had led me to believe to the contrary so far – that I had a brain and I could learn. It was an enormous boost to my confidence and happiness levels to be able to study in the way I wanted and choose topics that interested me. It was an experience that planted the seed of my support of the un-schooling movement that is spreading far and wide today.

I still kept my dream to travel and dance and I was convinced that I already knew everything there was to know about life. When I left college, I was ready to conquer the world. I had no idea how to go about getting a job in the heady world of show biz, only that I was going to. And I kept dreaming about it every day.

Chapter Six

KNOW WHAT YOU WANT, AND THE 'HOW' WILL APPEAR

Within a few months of leaving college, my dance teacher phoned up and said that a friend of a friend had called her with a job opportunity for a dancer in Italy. Someone had backed out of a show and, with only three weeks to go before the opening night, they were desperate to find a replacement. Within a week I had packed my bags, said goodbye to my family, and was sitting on a plane feeling desperately homesick and slightly shocked that what I had dreamed about was now a reality and I was about to become a professional dancer, just like Jackie Stevens.

I arrived at my new home at 2am in the morning after my flight had been diverted due to fog in Milan. There are two airports in Milan, Linate and Malpenza and I was due to land in Linate, a forty minute drive away from the guest house that was to be home for the next two months before the company went on tour. Unfortunately, the fog was so thick that we ended up landing in Malpenza airport, almost two hours drive from my final destination.

I had only been abroad twice in my life and that was just for family holidays, so I wasn't exactly a seasoned traveller and no doubt was daydreaming when they were making announcements. So, when we landed in Malpenza, I just assumed I would have to find my own way to Linate. Once I was clear of Customs, I got a train into the centre of Milan to save some money and from there, feeling very competent and grown-up, I got a taxi to Linate airport. I was excited about meeting the head dancer whom I knew was named Julie and was due to meet me at the airport. I envisioned us hitting it off straight away and chatting all the way back in the car, so I would be able to catch up on what they had done in rehearsals so far and find out who else was in the company. I was really looking forward to it and arrived at Linate airport excited and ready to meet my new friend.

Unfortunately, in 1983, mobile phones had yet to become a common item in one's handbag so I had no idea that fifteen minutes before, Julie had given up waiting and gone home. She was exhausted after five days of gruelling rehearsals, and wasn't exactly thrilled that she had been sent to meet me. When the transfer coach that I should have caught at Malpenza finally arrived without me on it, she had just assumed that I had bottled out and had headed for her bed. So of course when I arrived, there was nobody there to meet me. It all felt very unwelcoming and flat. It didn't take much investigation to realise what an idiotic thing I'd done by not simply getting on the transfer coach, like all the other people on my flight had done.

After staring open-mouthed at the man behind the information desk for longer than was appropriate, I found a bus that would take me back to the train station in the centre of Milan. I was running out of lire fast and didn't want to risk another taxi. Unlike my journey from Malpenza to Linate, this time I didn't meet anybody who spoke English. As my Italian was limited to 'Spaghetti Bolognaise per favore', I went into a daze and wandered around for a while, clutching the piece of paper that had my new address scribbled on it and trying to pull myself together.

I kept talking to myself: *If I get myself to a station close to this address, I will be okay. Don't think about home, don't cry, don't think about Mum and Dad, don't think about my sisters or our lovely warm house, don't think about my beautiful dog Scamp, don't cry.*

After finding an English-speaking student who was drunk and oblivious to my plight but helpful enough to put me on the right platform, I had a long, cold wait before I was finally on the train to my new life. I sat numbly looking out into the darkness of this new land. The train creaked along torturously slowly: *'what an idiot, what an idiot, what an idiot'* taunted the engine. Finally, with a dismissive snigger, it shuddered to a halt at Brescia station. I gave the last of my lire to an impatient cab driver, who had been openly disgruntled at the lack of tip and had disappeared as quickly as he could in the hope of finding a more generous client, and I found myself standing outside the guesthouse in the freezing, pitch-black December air, suitcase at my side, staring at the faint outline of the building that stood in front of me. Not a light was on in the house.

On the plane, I had imagined I would be met by a gaggle of excited dancers and we would party into the night, anticipating all the adventures to come. I guess there was a part of me that was still hoping... Any bit of residual optimism fizzled away as I knocked on the big wooden door. After hearing lots of shuffling and grumbling, a sleepy middle-aged woman opened it, half acknowledged me and then tutted and muttered to herself in Italian as she led me to the room I was to share with two other dancers. I choked back my tears. I wanted my mum there to cuddle me and sympathise about what an awful trip it had been; I wanted her to put me to bed and bring me hot chocolate and tuck me in. I dragged my suitcase up the stairs and crept quietly into the room she had indicated before shuffling back down the stairs and no doubt back to her bed.

As the dim light from the corridor slipped into the darkened room, I could make out three beds in a row. The two on the edges were occupied. A sleepy mop of curls raised her head, pointed to the bed in the middle and said, "See you in the morning," before flopping back onto the pillow. It was so cold that I just took off my shoes and got under the covers fully dressed. I had never wanted to be back in the house I grew up in more than in that moment; even more than the first time I went away from home on a Girl Guide camping trip when I was eleven. That time, I was so homesick and stressed once it went dark that I wet my sleeping bag the first night and spent the next two nights in a damp bag, praying nobody would find out. As I lay in my strange cold Italian bed I desperately wanted to be a child again, safely cradled in the bosom of my family. Leaving home was cold, scary and horrible.

It was starting to get light when I drifted off to sleep, wishing with all my might that I would wake up back home in the room I shared with my younger sister, with that wonderful sense of relief you feel when you wake from a bad dream. I woke with the covers still pulled over my head; the two girls were talking as they got ready for rehearsal. I bit my lip as the tears came. I didn't want to be here.

Before I had a chance to wallow, I sat up. "Hi," I said feebly. "I got lost last night."

"Oh, you poor thing. We were really worried about you and then just assumed you had changed your mind and stayed in England. I'm Claire, by the way. Sorry I couldn't say much last night but I was *soooooo* tired after yesterday's rehearsal. The choreographer is a demon, but it's brilliant work. You'd better get unpacked and ready. He'll be furious if we're late."

Claire was certainly making up for her lack of conversation the night before. Within a few minutes, I learned that there were another three girls in the next room and we were a company of six dancers and our show was to open in ten days and I had a week's rehearsal to catch up on. Three of the girls were the same age as me, nineteen, two were eighteen and one was twenty. There was so much to do that morning, I didn't have time to be homesick. At breakfast, I was greeted warmly by the grumpy guesthouse owner from the night before and witnessed the other girls conversing with their broken Italian. I was impressed. Everything was new and interesting. The old guest house, the food, the language, the smells. I was beginning to feel glad again that I was a grown-up and excited by the journey I had stepped into.

After breakfast, we walked over to the studio space that happened to be just across the street. We were met by a handsome Argentinian choreographer. I felt quite shy at first as I had only ever had female dance teachers before. Esteban was stern and authoritative. Although there was a sparkle in his eye, he clearly loved the power of being able to tell six young girls what to do. He took full advantage of our youth and vulnerability and worked us like slaves. I loved it!

I loved waking up every morning and rolling out of bed with every inch of me aching, from the ends of my hair to the tips of my toes. I loved the new choreography. It was so different from anything I had ever done before. It was powerful and required strength and agility, as well as being graceful and slick. I learnt so much in that first job, which was a cabaret show with strong elements of contemporary dance. By the time the contract came to an end six months later, my body was sculpted and strong and I felt like I had finally earned the credit of being a 'good' dancer'.

For a good seven or eight years after that first contract, work came in easily. I rarely auditioned, as there was usually a new job waiting as one ended. I have always been a bit of a hopper, getting bored quickly with structure and predictability, so this was the perfect job for me. It allowed me to see the world, work with different choreographers and meet new people. I loved landing in a new country, feeling the heat hit my face as I stepped out of the plane, or the cold, dry smell of snow, knowing that this strange land was slowly going to become home and create feelings of nostalgia in the future, when I stumbled upon a familiar taste or smell that would transport me back to this exciting time in my life. It wasn't always rosy; there were difficult relationships, poorly paid jobs that barely paid the rent, in fact, I remember at one point, when I was living in a guest house with no self catering facilities I was so broke, I heated baked beans up on a travel iron for a couple of nights to serve as my evening meal! There were places that I didn't like, relationships that ended badly, times that I felt homesick and wanted to pack it all in. But on the whole, life was fresh and exciting and it was good to be young and out in the world.

Chapter Seven

BACK TO BLIGHTY

I was in my mid twenties and had just finished a long stint in Israel when I first experienced the well-known pitfalls of the profession.

Once my contract in Israel had come to an end, I went to stay in London with my friend Bev, a dancer I had worked with a few years before in Italy. This was something I often did inbetween jobs. I usually only stayed a week or so before I was off on another contract.

However, this time I had a few unfruitful months. There wasn't much work on offer and I flunked quite a few auditions. I was beginning to feel that I was outstaying my welcome at Bev's, after eight weeks of what should have been a couple of weeks' stay.

Finally, I was offered a contract travelling in Hong Kong, Taiwan and Japan for eight months. I hadn't enjoyed the audition; the choreography was basic and, quite frankly, boring. In the past, I wouldn't have taken a contract this long unless I loved the choreography but, for the first time, I broke my own rule with the excuse that this was a good opportunity to see the Far East. There is something about breaking your own rules that chips away at your self esteem and self trust and, although I enjoyed seeing those wonderful places and had a lot of fun, I soon regretted the decision. For the first time since I became a professional dancer, I was bored with the show and performed on automatic pilot. Once the contract was over, I returned to London feeling slightly jaded and uninspired.

It was certainly true for me that, when I was younger, I couldn't see how the decisions I made on a day-to-day basis were creating my future. Neither did I understand that my life as it was, had been created by the decisions I had made in the past, all influenced and intermingled by the people I encountered and the experiences I had along the way. The weaver is always at work; with every thought we have and every move we make, we create the tapestry of our story. Little did I realise at that point that my life, through my own making, was beginning to change its course.

I was beginning to yearn for something more, of what I wasn't sure, but somehow life wasn't quite as satisfying as it had been. I hadn't found Mr Right yet and although I wanted a stable relationship, it wasn't really that high on my agenda. In fact, the thought of settling down and having a family like my sisters didn't appeal to me at all. I didn't doubt that I would do it one day and I never had any worries about leaving it too late; after all, I was only twenty-seven, I just thought it would happen when I was ready. I was getting bored with moving around and although I wasn't quite ready to stop dancing, feelings of insecurity about the future were creeping up on me. The thought of disappearing off the dance scene and doing a boring run-of-the-mill job terrified me. I didn't want to be a dance teacher, either, as staying in the same room week in, week out, teaching a set syllabus just didn't appeal. I had worked as a choreographer for a while when I was in Israel and really enjoyed it. I didn't know that much about the professional world of choreography, except of course that it was '*a hard profession to get into*', but I felt I would like to explore it more.

I decided it was time to stop travelling and try and make some contacts in London. It was also during this period that it became more obvious that I was struggling with my health. My childhood asthma had been slowly creeping up on me since my mid-twenties and, after a bad chest infection that kept me off work for a week and a course of super-strong antibiotics, asthma became a permanent feature in my life. Instead of a slight, niggling condition I had had as a child, I found that I used an inhaler more and more frequently and felt unable cope if I didn't have it with me.

My usual accommodation at Bev's was already occupied, so I sought out my good friend Graham and stayed on his couch for a while. We had met five years earlier when we were both working at a theme pub on the outskirts of London. At the time, I was waiting for confirmation of a visa so I could join a theatre company in Israel and, in the meantime, Bev offered me the perfect job – as a dancing barmaid!

She was working as a choreographer in a pub with a horseshoe-shaped bar in the middle that doubled up as a stage. The floor was raised behind the bar, making it knee height on the staff side and chest height on the punters' side. The bar staff were made up of twelve dancers, who doubled up as bar staff. Several times throughout the evening we would nip off, change costume and then burst back onto the transformed stage (which meant drinks had stopped being served and any spillage had been mopped up!). We would perform a show-stopping, high energy, big West End number, soak up the rapturous applause and then carry on serving in our latest costumes, until our cue came for us to run backstage and change, ready for the next mind-blowing number.

I worked there for three months and each month we would focus on a different show. The first month, the theme was *The Dreamgirls* musical, the second month fell around Christmas so we did a tribute to Pantomime, and the third month was *West Side Story*. In between the shows, Graham, the resident DJ, would keep the party going with the latest tunes. It was during the after-show drinks that Graham and I became friends.

I really enjoyed the job. The idea was novel and the first two months worked brilliantly. There was always a lively crowd present, the choreography was interesting and challenging enough and I enjoyed the social side of bar work. The only problem was that the owner had a slightly different agenda. Now, bearing in mind that the venue wasn't in the most salubrious of areas and was a pub, the best approach was to keep it lively, the dance numbers relatively short and high energy and the bar open as much as possible. This balance was kept perfectly in the first two months and made the pub hugely successful. However, as time went on, Dennis, the owner, revealed more and more of his obsession to be a West End producer and performer.

Rehearsals for month three started and we all bundled into the pub at 10am, a bit grumpy and tired after working until late the night before. We changed into rehearsal clothes and warmed up whilst we waited for Bev, the choreographer, to tell us all about the theme of the month.

Bev walked in about an hour later, rolling her eyes and pulling a face and mouthing, "Oh my." Behind her, beaming from ear to ear, strutted Dennis. He spent the morning proudly going through the plans for month three, the theme of which would be *West Side Story*. Only this time we would do the whole story, which he would narrate.

"Nice idea, but how are we going to keep the bar open, and the party atmosphere, *and* do a full blown musical?"

Of course nobody actually verbalised those thoughts to Dennis, we were all too scared of losing our jobs. Instead, we kept quiet, rehearsed hard in the day, and did our bickering whilst we changed from Widow Twanky into Aladdin costumes at night.

As the rehearsal period went on, Dennis's bits of narration got longer and longer and we seemed to be in Freeze position far more than was necessary. He also decided that the death scene at the end needed to be more drawn out and dramatic, so it was concluded that Maria would mime her heartbreak as he narrated.

"Oh my!" became the catchphrase amongst the dancers.

Opening night dawned. The pub had been transformed into the set of *West Side Story* with the use of scaffolding and backdrops. In fact, it looked pretty impressive and really suited the venue. The punters arrived in high spirits, most of them regulars and looking forward to what we had in store for them this month.

It started off well and in the usual fashion. A few snappy, high-energy numbers, good choreography and costumes and the audience were enjoying it. However, as the evening progressed it was clear that the bar was shutting down more often and the 'show bits,' which were usually a breath of fresh air and a burst of energy, were getting a bit tedious and long. Dennis, on the other hand, was thoroughly enjoying himself, improvising, adding the odd joke here and there, making his epic script even longer. We froze dutifully in our poses, becoming more and more irritated and embarrassed. We could hear the comments from the audience:

"Come on, get on with it."

"Me beer's gone warm, darlin'."

"Bleedin' shite this month, innit?"

Dennis was in his own world, mesmerised by the sound of his own voice. He was on stage, living his dream and nothing else mattered. It was amazing how he didn't even notice the increase in volume of general crowd noise, indicating that nobody was bloody listening. To the crowd, we were just a bunch of annoying prima donnas that kept shutting the bar down to show off!

In between the performances, Dennis retired to his dressing room and we pulled pints for the depleting crowds. It was depressing. The ones that had managed to get enough alcohol down them were much more blunt about how crap the new show was; some were downright aggressive and rude, making us all feel on edge. It was even harder to deal with the nicer customers, who felt sorry for us and were hanging in there as moral support when we knew they couldn't wait to get out and most certainly wouldn't be back this month, if at all.

The grand finale finally came and it began with a great show-stopping number which actually managed to lift the spirit of the room, most probably helped by the fact that people had got wise by now and had stocked up on their poison when the bar was open. Unfortunately, the number was followed by 'the stabbing', which led to Maria, prompted by Dennis's narration, miming her heartbreak. The backing track turned slow and mournful. I had decided that no matter what, I would be professional and stick to what I was here to do. I threw myself into my final dramatic freeze, which was leaning over the bar overcome with grief, unable witness the pain of my sister Maria.

"Two gin and tonics and a bag of dried roasted please, love." A punter had staggered over to me, oblivious to the fact I was in the throes of a dramatic performance.

"'Scuse me, love," she slurred

I felt irritated. Couldn't this stupid woman see I was in character? She tapped me on my back. I threw my head up dramatically and stared in horror at my sister Maria, who was slumped over the body of the love she had just lost forever and then buried my head in my hands.

"Do you work 'ere or not?"

"I'm busy." I threw the words out of the side of my mouth

"You don't look it to me, darlin'."

"I'm acting!" I was outraged

"Yer what?"

"Sod off!" I was failing to keep my focus

I saw her tottering over to my friend Garry, who was in a similar pose to me further down the bar. I moved my head so I could watch as she ordered from him. I saw his body start to shake and he buried his head further into his shirt. He'd lost it and I suddenly saw the other side of this pathetic situation and, feeling myself surrender any remnants of pride for the whole sorry scene, I wept with laughter.

It got worse as the music faded and I heard Garry snort unbelievably loudly, making Dennis fluff his lines. It was no use, my self-control had deserted me and it was time for us all to stand up and slowly, one by one, say our goodbyes to our dear departed friend. I lifted my head and tried to arrange my laughing face into some kind of contorted shock and grief. My eyes accidentally met Garry's and a delighted shriek flew out of my mouth. Dennis glared at me furiously but I just couldn't get it together. I spent a few desperate moments trying to pretend I was acting really hard and had chosen to go mad with grief, before finally admitting to myself that there was no way I could carry on.

As I walked off the stage, I felt Garry closely at my heels. At least we were trying to walk off slowly! Once backstage, we threw ourselves onto the floor and howled with laughter. The relief was tremendous. We scuttled back to serve drinks as soon as the show was over and spent the rest of the evening avoiding Dennis, who thankfully stormed off to dinner with his doting mother.

That evening, Garry and I struck up a friendship of the sort that is inevitably created by sharing such hysterical historical events. Thankfully, my visa came through for Israel a few days later.

A year later, I was still in Israel and when I was offered work choreographing for a dance company, I contacted Garry and offered him a job as a dancer. He had since started a relationship with Graham and, when Garry accepted my invitation, the ever-resourceful Graham created a character called Ruby Relish, donned a wig, dress and heels, formed an unusual act with a French contortionist and found himself work out in Israel as a cabaret artist. We became good friends whilst we were living in this complex and beautiful country and stayed in touch once our time there was over.

I had only been staying with Graham in London for a few weeks when I auditioned for the London Monarchs. An American company wanted to bring American football to Europe and they were looking for dancers to form England's first ever-professional cheerleading squad.

I went along feeling unenthused but ready to give anything a chance. I didn't want to be a fluffy bit of candy, shaking pom-poms and grinning and chewing gum as I yelled out support for a sport I knew nothing about. But I was out of work and unfit and there wasn't much else on offer, so I put some dance clothes in a bag and, without much thought, took a tube to the Hippodrome in Leicester Square. To my surprise, the place was packed. I learned later that four hundred girls had auditioned that day, something that meant a lot because, as it turned out, I was one of the twenty lucky dancers that were offered a place in the squad.

It was about twenty minutes into the audition that I decided I really wanted the job. I never realised how hard cheerleaders worked. The pace was fast, the energy was high and fun and the choreography was certainly challenging enough. The audition pushed me to my limit physically, which was something I needed after my stint in the Far East. Being an American project, there was also loads of hype, big radio mikes, TV cameras, lots of business people in suits hanging around the sides looking important and a large audition panel. It was noisy and vibrant and I soon got swept away with the glamour and the competitive atmosphere. I was very happy to get through round after round and finally be picked to be part of the squad. It was just the tonic I needed!

I was a Crown Jewel cheerleader for the London Monarchs for two years and it was the perfect job. The first season was a dream. It lasted from March to September and, with big money behind getting American Football to Europe, we did TV shows, radio interviews, photo shoots, even made a record! We got flown to New York and chauffeured around in limousines and performed in the Giants Stadium. Our home games were beyond exciting and memories of running out onto the pitch at Wembley Stadium to a roaring crowd of fifty thousand people still sends a shiver down my spine. We got invited to great parties and functions, met lots of celebrities, and even danced with Take That! It was all larger than life and I threw myself into it with gusto!

Once the first season ended, I decided to stay in London. I had acquired my first home by then and was sharing a flat in West Dulwich with Sarah, whom I had met working behind the food bar at Jongleurs comedy club whilst I was rehearsing for the Crown Jewels. As I knew the audition for the second season would come around in six months' time, I decided to stay put in the flat and work the winter at Jongleurs. I also used the winter to qualify as a fitness instructor. London was an expensive place to live and being a fitness instructor meant much better pay, a chance to stay fit and better hours, so I could still manage to get to auditions and do the odd dance class. Through being a fitness instructor, I also learned valuable lessons in how to teach and present, something I didn't really appreciate until years later.

When the second season for the London Monarchs came around, I was delighted to pass the audition again, but the experience of being a Crown Jewel was completely different by then. The main backers had pulled out and the glamour went with them. The actual dance work was still good, but, without the hype, it seemed like hard graft for very little returns and the job certainly didn't hold the status it had the year before. I hung on until the end of the season and it was a real come-down. If I had followed my instinct, I would have pulled out, but I plumped for having a regular income for a few more months. It all felt pretty sad and soul-destroying, like roaming around in the debris after a party. Crowds had dwindled and the atmosphere at the games was flat. My health was also becoming more and more of a problem. It was a nagging concern that I did my best to ignore, but it kept digging me in the ribs.

I went to the doctor's a few times with my concerns about the amount of Ventolin I needed to take in order to get through the day. It felt wrong to have to rely on spraying drugs into my lungs in order to be able to achieve what should be a perfectly natural function. The doctor's answer was always to "up the dose". I was also embarrassed about my condition and hid it as much as I could. I was a dancer and fitness instructor, I was supposed to be in the peak of physical health and constantly wheezing and coughing didn't fit with the image I wanted people to have of me! I hung a lot on my image in those days.

I felt lost and confused by the apparent downturn in my luck. I guess it was my silent call for change that drew to me an ego-denting experience, that turned out to be a catalyst for my long, but fruitful search for a deeper experience of being human.

Chapter Eight

AND THE WINNER IS...

I was scanning the job section of *The Stage* newspaper on my way to teach an aerobic class in the centre of London, when I saw a huge advert calling all dancers to an audition for the West End musical *Starlight Express* that day, starting at 10am. If I raced out once I had finished teaching, I would probably get there in time. At the bottom, it said *Bring sheet music*.

This would normally have put me off. I wasn't a singer, I had never had any formal voice training and I wasn't particularly confident with my voice. However, when I was in Japan, karaoke, which was unheard of in England at that time, was extremely popular. In fact, it was hard to find a bar that didn't feature karaoke. Each night after our show, we would inevitably end up in one of these joints and, after a few drinks I'd pluck up the courage to sing. The only drawback was that the words were all in Japanese and the only song I vaguely knew the words to were *Moon River*. So, every night at some point, just like the pub drunk, I would ask for the microphone and hiccough my way through *Moon River*.

The Japanese are an extremely polite race and they would applaud sincerely at the end and tell me I had a beautiful voice. My hazy, drunken memory came back to me that morning and I decided that if I was good enough for the Japanese – and I was good, they told me so every night – I was good enough for *Starlight Express*. I jumped off the tube and ran into a music shop that was close by, quickly flicked through the sheet music and found *Moon River* within seconds. A sign! It was meant to be. I snatched it out of the rack, ran to the till, thrust the money at the bored-looking woman behind it and ran to get my class over and done with.

I arrived at the audition at 10.30am, bright red and puffing and panting. I ran straight to the toilets, pulled out my inhaler and sprayed double the dose down my throat, sucking it deeply into my lungs and willing myself to calm down. I changed as quickly as my sweaty skin and shaky, Ventolin-filled body would let me and ran into the audition hall. There, my heart sank into my feet. There must have been about another two hundred and fifty girls there at least and I knew they only wanted four!

I walked over to register, telling myself I had just as much chance as anyone else, although my hopes of even getting through the first round were quickly diminishing. I handed in my CV and contact details and in return was given my number 296. 296! There were even more dancers here than I had guessed and there were still more girls queuing up behind me to register. We hung around for another half hour or so. It was nerve-racking, to say the least. I did my usual trick of keeping my eyes focused on the floor. I didn't want what little confidence

I had left to die, so it was best to avoid checking out the competition altogether.

We started to learn the routine. I have never had the knack of learning anything quickly and choreography was no exception. In auditions, I would have to concentrate really hard to learn the routine and go over and over the steps when the choreographer grabbed a drink, or had a quick chat with the director. I found them frustrating and exhausting and this one was doubly so. The room was too small to accommodate the crowd comfortably; in fact, it was so packed, it was difficult to even see the choreographer properly, let alone have room to move. Girls were belting each other, standing on each other's toes, tutting and complaining. It was a cattle market.

After about twenty minutes, we had learned sixteen bars' worth of choreography and were told to get into groups of twenty. I kept practising the routine and kept my head down. Our group was about fifteenth to go and I stepped forward quickly when we were called, to make sure I got a place in the front line so I could be seen properly. There was an audition panel of about ten people and I guessed that they were allocated to watch two people each.

The intro started and I hit my starting position, right arm up, left hand on hip, legs in jazz second and head held high. I counted in the intro and we were off. I stuck a big West End-style smile on my face and threw myself into the choreography like a woman possessed. The minute or so went by in a blur and before I knew it, I was holding the end position. Deep, groin-aching lunge, arms out wide and head thrown towards the gods. It felt as if we were there for hours, the silence only broken by the desperate breath pattern of twenty girls having just risked their lives to get on a West End stage.

"Thank you." The choreographer's voice gave us the cue to release the posture and look normal again. And then, as always, the worst bit: "Stay where you are for now and in a few moments we will call out the numbers of those of you we would like to stay."

I looked at my feet and listened to the sound of my heartbeat racing, staring at the sweat that dripped off my chin and onto the floor in front of me as I concentrated all my strength and mental power into one thought: *Please, oh please, say 296. 296! Come on, say it, 296. Let me be in those lucky numbers, please!*

The choreographer's voice boomed in to the room once again.

"Okay, the numbers we would like to stay for the next round are 280, 285, 289, 291, 293 and 296. Thanks to those who we haven't asked to stay, you are free to go. Next group, please!"

Relief flooded my whole body. I had got through to the next round! I went straight to the back of the room and went over and over the routine. Round Two came around about thirty minutes later. I made it through again! I went to the back and practised, kept my eyes down and stayed focused. Something was working and I was getting through. Round Three came and a stunning performance by myself led to hearing my magical number being called yet again. It was a fantastic feeling of achievement. Boy, it was good to be a winner. Lately, life had felt like a swim uphill in a lead coat, and it was good to have some respite. The pressure was on and I was happy to be amongst it.

Round Four was the final round of dance before they would ask us to sing. Come on, *Moon River*, we can do this together! We were down to about sixty dancers now, so we were split into groups of ten. The audition had been going on for three hours, we were exhausted and the room was moist with sweat and smelt like a sauna full of dirty laundry that had been sprayed with fifteen different types of deodorant. The sweet smell of success! I loved it. This was show biz at its best, the hardship, the humiliation, the toil and tears. I felt as proud as punch to have made it this far.

We went in to the final round and I danced like I had never danced before. I felt as light as a feather, the music swept me away and the dance danced itself. At last, the thirty numbers were announced. Mine was first! In a daze, I drifted over to my bag, my feet barely touching the floor. I pulled out my towel, added another brand of deodorant to the toxic concoction around me and sat down to go over the words of my song. This was great. I was called out first, so I would no doubt sing first. I was so pumped with adrenalin and confidence, I felt I could take on the world. Although I had never sung at an audition, I knew I could make it through feeling the way I did now.

As the other disappointed auditionees drifted unhappily away, we, (the potential stars of the future), were called to the centre of the room.

"The singing auditions will be held in the music room next door. We will call you in one by one in numerical order, so you can decide now whether to eat lunch or not."

I checked out the numbers stuck onto the chests of the others and realised that I would be last. Which meant at

least a one and a half hour wait. Shit! There was nothing
I could do, so I just had to keep reminding myself of how
lucky I had been so far today. I was through, wasn't I? I
had been chosen over hundreds to sing. I could do this;
after all, I had done it before. I toyed with the idea of
going to the pub and getting plastered, as it was the only
state I had ever sung in, in public, but I decided against
it. I would just have to keep faith in myself, go in there
and give it my all.

I sat in the corner, head lowered and took out my
sandwich. I was starving. The bit of jam on toast I had
stuffed down that morning was hardly enough fuel for
an aerobics class and four hours of adrenalin-sucking
auditioning. I bit into it and felt sick. I was too wired to
enjoy it so I stuffed it back in my bag and picked up my
sheet music. After an hour, I had read my words at least
thirty times, put on a fifth layer of lipstick, changed my
hair style umpteen times and made three further attempts
to eat my sandwich. All this was interspersed with
attempts to copy the voice warm-ups the other girls were
doing, whilst trying to block out how good they all
sounded.

My nerves were mounting again and I foolishly
decided to do what I now consider to be auditionee
suicide; I popped into the corridor to see how the singing
auditions were going. The door to the music room was
slightly open and I could hear the introduction of a well-
known song from *Chorus Line*. I reached the tiny
window at the top of the door in time to see a girl swing
around to face the auditioning committee and burst into:

"*Tits and ass.*
Where the cupboard once was bare,
Now you knock and someone's there."

She was brilliant! Her voice was powerful and strong. She strutted about the room like she owned the place! I felt the bottom drop out of my world. I hadn't even considered *how* I would sing my song. I guess my usual visual accompaniment, which was me sitting slumped on a bar stool, wasn't going to cut the mustard with these guys. I pulled myself away and went back to the studio to discreetly rehearse a few moves. *Moon* and *River* didn't give me much inspiration and I decided to just go in there and belt it out.

"Number 296, please."

Phew! Finally, it was my turn. I was the only one left in the huge dance studio. I picked up my bag and sheet music and walked into the music room. Seven tired, pale faces smiled weakly at me from behind a long table at the end of the surprisingly large room. It had been a long day for all of us. A piano stood in the corner with a bored-looking pianist behind it. He placed my copy of *Moon River* on the music stand and I walked confidently into the centre of the room, legs like jelly and bile in my throat. I turned around, ready to blast them with my voice, blow them away with my soulful rendition of this classic piece.

"What key?" The pianist's unexpected voice made me jump.

"What *what*?" I said

"What key do you want me to play in?" he repeated, making no effort to hide his lack of enthusiasm.

Shit! I didn't know, I had no idea what key I sung in and it had never even crossed my mind to find out.

"Err… C," I said authoritatively. *That should be okay*, I comforted myself. *I think that's the general one.*

The intro started and I pulled myself up to full height, fixed my eyes just above the audition panel and took a deep breath – and heard my voice flop weakly into the room.

"Moon River, wider than a mile,
I'm crossing you in style some day…"
Keep going, keep going, I told myself, *you can sing better than this, it'll come. At least you've chosen the right key.*

Just as I thought that, the key plummeted
"Old dream maker…"
I pushed my chin down and sunk into my diaphragm to reach the notes I needed and heard this awful drone come out of the bowels of my voice box. Oh God, I'd forgotten about that drop. I pushed on.
"… You heartbreaker…"
Thank goodness it was going up again.
"Wherever you're going, I'm going your way."
I made the awful mistake of letting my eyes glance down to the face of the woman directly in front of me. It was contorted with suppressed laughter. As our eyes met, she looked fleetingly horrified, grabbed a tissue from the box in front of her and, pretending to blow her nose, buried her whole face into it. Her body shook, she was hysterical. I froze and willed my eyes not to look at anyone else. I tried to focus them back above her head but I was like a rabbit caught in headlights.

Mortified and purple with shame, I somehow still managed to keep the offensive rendition of this great classic going to the bitter end. When I finished, I stood staring at the floor. The silence was deafening. I knew no one dared speak for fear of shrieking with laughter.

And then, and for some reason – and this was the most painful bit – I betrayed myself even more by uttering the words, "Sorry about that." There was a long pause.

"Thank you, you can go now and we will be in touch by letter," a shaky voice replied.

Eyes firmly fixed on the floor, I walked across to the exit, the sound of my footsteps bouncing off the walls of the empty room. I felt like an ugly, stupid, talent-less giant. I reached the door and put my hand out to push it open.

"Excuse me."

I spun round hopefully in a knee-jerk reaction and saw seven flushed faces, eyes shining, mouths curved in their efforts to keep their faces straight.

"You forgot your sheet music."

I then had to walk back across the room, footsteps now sounding like I had on the outfit of a one man band, past the audition panel who I knew were following my every move and over to the piano to retrieve my music. I then had to repeat the traumatic journey all the way back to the door.

Bastards! I silently cursed. *Cruel, heartless bastards, how dare you! You could have just let me leave*. What hurt the most was that I knew that the moment I was out of that door and out of earshot, they would collapse into laughter. I had no doubt about it. I could just see them, clutching onto each other with uncontrollable hysteria, enjoying the biggest laugh of their lives. All at my expense.

I grabbed my stuff and shot out of the building as quickly as I could, cringing all the way back to the flat I shared in West Dulwich. I spent the whole journey trying to block the miserable day out of my mind. How was it possible to experience so much joy and humiliation in one day? Life sucked! I went straight to bed when I got back and stayed there for a week and a half with a chest infection.

Chapter Nine

TURNING POINT

It was about two weeks after my audition of shame that my long-suffering friend and flatmate pointed me in a direction that eventually changed my life and career completely. I had come home yet again in a foul mood after what was fast becoming a typical day, which consisted of failing an audition and then going on to my crap job in a trendy health club. Wearing the customary skin-tight leggings and leotard, hair in a really high tight ponytail to give me that 'Whey hey! Isn't life just *soooo* amazing when you're super fit?' look, I would inhale a massive dose of Ventolin, put my best, fun-kinda gal personality on show and throw myself into an hour and fifteen minutes performance of jumping jacks, knees-ups, jumps on the spot and 'you name it, I'll do it to pay the rent' groovy moves, all the time whooping, shrieking, hollering and grinning like a Barbie doll possessed.

I would then sulk, mutter and scowl all the way back to the flat in West Dulwich and proceed to rant at Sarah about how the world was against me, it wasn't fair, I worked really hard and was still going into debt, how I hated my job and I had to endure yet another humiliating audition where all the shit people got picked AGAIN, no doubt they had slept with the choreographer, blah blah blah.

No doubt Sarah would brace herself when she heard my key in the door every night and was probably wondering whether she should offer me her homoeopath's number or punch me in the gob. Thankfully her kinder side got the better of her.

"A whatoeopath?" I stared at her in disbelief. What could this homoeo-thingy do to get me a job and cure me of this dreaded curse that was inflicted upon me by a cruel and unjust world?

"A homoeopath," repeated Sara patiently. "There's her number if you want to call her, she may help you get to the bottom of your, err… health problems." ("*And hopefully cure you of your self-indulgent whining and save your dear friend from serving a life sentence in prison*",) she no doubt added under her breath as she closed the door of her bedroom. She seemed to spend a lot of time in there in those days.

After a few more weeks of torturous life as I had come to know it, I decided to take Sarah's advice and make an appointment with the homoeopath.

I rang the bell of the clinic in Camden and Ena, a motherly-looking woman with a kind face, opened up the door. She invited me into her room, which was homely and warm. After taking down my details, she raised her eyes and I felt like she was looking straight into me.

"So, Lianne…" Her soft Irish accent sounded safe and wise. "Tell me about yourself. What was life like for you as a child?"

"What?"

I wasn't expecting this. What did she mean, what was I like as a child? I wasn't here for a chat. I wanted to talk about my health, get some pills and bog off! Not wanting to be rude, though, I started to talk…

Two hours later, I bounced onto the street having talked, laughed and cried myself into a state of lightness and hope. It was amazing. For the first time ever, I had sat with a health professional and felt like *I* was the authority. I was asked questions, rather than being told things, I was listened to, not talked at, and I was left to speak without interruption. I felt respected and more in control of my health than I had ever been.

And, to this day, I am still grateful to Sarah for choosing not to smack me in the gob.

My visit to Ena planted a seed, or rather several seeds, of different ways of looking at life. Maybe it wasn't just rotten luck and a random poor constitution that was creating my ill health. Maybe my emotions, experiences and attitude to life, had something to do with it. I also realised that this wasn't the first time I had been presented with this idea. A few other people had been hinting lately. Only the previous week, my best friend Cathy had been enthusiastically telling me about a book she was reading that was all about how we create our day with our thoughts. I vaguely remembered her babbling on about manifesting parking spaces and feeling gratitude, as I sulked my way through a second piece of cheesecake after a strenuous workout in the gym.

I also recalled a morning at home when I was moaning about putting weight on. Instead of a giving me a hug or a sympathetic whine back, Sara asked me, "Why do you think you are putting weight on? Do you want to be noticed? Or do you feel you need the protection? Are you punishing yourself?"

I had stared at her open-mouthed, as if she had just spoken to me in some obscure German dialect.

"'Cos I like chips," was my flippant reply, as I flounced out of the door feeling rather pleased with my dismissive response. "New age bollocks," I remember muttering to myself.

I greeted Cathy with "Sorry, sorry and sorry" as we sat down to lunch in the café where we worked as fitness instructors.

"What for?" Cathy asked, cheerful as ever.

I filled her in on my realisation. Cathy looked at me with a mixture of affection and relief. "What was that book you were telling me about?" I asked.

Cathy needed no more prompting and spent the rest of lunch gushing over how amazing it was. This time, I listened and on the way home I nipped into a bookshop in Covent Garden and bought the book, *Living Magically*, by Gill Edwards. I read the title and felt excited, which was a rare experience on a cramped train on a wet Monday evening. Then I dived into the first page and a new chapter of my life.

The book gave me a complete re-frame of my view of life, by suggesting that we create what we need even if it doesn't seem like we need it. The way we think and feel is reflected in our life experiences and there are lessons to be learned in every situation. As I read on, I was encouraged to live my life magically and see everything life has to offer as a wonderful gift, guiding me to the next step of my evolution. According to Gill, the more we choose this approach, the less we need to grow through struggle. Life becomes joyful and full of wonder.

As I read more, I felt as if someone was wiping the windows to my world clean. The book resonated with me at a very deep level. I wasn't a victim of circumstance, I was a participant, I had a say in the way things turned out. Along with this 'ah-ha' moment came a squirming sensation as I began to realise what a pain in the arse I had become, so negative about life and so angry. No wonder I was attracting such bad luck when all I did was moan and blame! It's funny how a little bit of knowledge can completely swing things around as a different perspective presents itself.

As I pondered on the twists and turns my life had taken, it became clearer why certain things had turned out the way they had. It also raised more questions than answers. I could see that for at least the first eight years of my career, I was in blissful ignorance. I was full of the confidence of youth and the expectation that things would go my way. I never doubted that I would get work as a dancer, after deciding I was following in Jackie Steven's footsteps and, once I experienced walking into my first job, I just knew I was doing what I was meant to do and, at the end of each contract there was nearly always another job offered to me. I rarely had to audition and the work was varied, sometimes with challenging choreography in fabulous theatres and venues with good pay, from time to time a television show and sometimes cabaret work or a small dance company that barely covered the rent. But it was fun and fulfilling and work came along easily.

Doubt started to creep in when I decided to stop travelling and put roots down in London. Although I got work and enjoyed being a Crown Jewel, along with a few trade shows and bits and bobs, I never felt that secure. I was often with girls who had been to stage school and seemed so much more sophisticated than me and the comments I had heard from well-meaning people when I was growing up kept rearing their ugly heads: "A dancer? It's a tough profession, you know"; "You'll never make a decent living doing that"; "There is too much competition, just keep it as a hobby"; "So many people fail in that industry". I could see how the rise of my doubts went hand in hand with the decline of opportunities for work and more and more experiences of being told, "No, thank you".

As the windows to my life got clearer, I felt a new surge of positive energy rising in me. I felt powerful again, and ready to take control by being responsible for my life. I wanted to know more and more about this wonderful way to live, these ancient secrets that opened up the mysteries of life.

With a strange feeling of pain and relief, I admitted to myself that although part of me was still thriving on the competition and achievement, there was a bigger part of me that knew this was a road to hell. I only felt good about myself when I was working, when I had a job I could be proud of, a job that meant I had been chosen above the rest. It wasn't that it was wrong to enjoy this exciting career, it was more that I depended so much on it in order to be happy, and my happiness relied so heavily on my identity. It was clear that my body wanted out of this competitive, approval-seeking existence. However, at that point, I knew nothing else.

I didn't know how to get back to doing it just for the love of it, as I was so conditioned to need approval. For all my attempts to be different and live my own life in the way I wanted, I was complying beautifully to the authority outside of myself. I was the perfectly predictable wild child. I conformed nicely by rejecting a 'normal' career, partied, took drugs, drank too much, looked suitably sulky, followed fashion and desperately wanted to be noticed and validated. And boy, had it caught up with me. My soul was calling out for more and the realisation was dawning that I wasn't going to find it 'out there'.

Chapter Ten

UP SHIT CREEK WITHOUT A PADDLE

True to my enthusiastic nature, over the next few years I dived headfirst into my new way of being. Unfortunately, I didn't stop to collect snorkel, flippers or oxygen tank, which led to many wrong turns and sticky situations. I ran like a bull in a china shop into every workshop I could find, jumped readily and trustingly onto the couch of anybody who so much as hinted that they were a healer and read every mind, body and soul book I could get my hands on, all the while preaching at every given opportunity to anyone who had a pair of ears. In short, I became a born-again lunatic, all in the name of finding everlasting health and happiness.

I experimented with crystal healing, acupuncture, Qi Gong, sound healing, speaking in tongues, visualisation, astrology, affirmations, radical diets and meditation. You name it and I have dabbled. Unfortunately, for the first three years at least, I was so excited and busy learning about this new world that I failed to put any of it into serious practice. I knew everything there was to know about how to change your life and be the master of your own destiny. I understood how yoga worked, the benefits of meditation and all about the energy body and I was still exhausted, unlucky and downright disillusioned.

I failed to realise that I was driven by fear. I was frightened of being ill. I was frightened by the prospect of having to give up dancing. Dancing was my whole identity and without it I was nothing, and fear drove me to find a way to cling onto it. I had lots of different experiences, some weird, some wonderful and some plain ridiculous. 'Aim for the moon and if you miss, you'll land among the stars' was my motto, and some of those stars sure were spiky!

I was browsing through the Mysteries bookstore in Covent Garden when I came across a flyer introducing me to 'Stargazer, healer of mind body and soul'. I read on and was hooked. It seemed all I had to do was go and see this woman, tap into this ancient vibration and everything else would be sorted. I was on the phone in a flash. She had a surprisingly free clinic considering her powers, but that escaped my notice.

Her 'healing temple' was her front room, which was a thirty-minute tube ride and a half hour walk away. I arrived wheezing and coughing and Stargazer, a dramatic, eagle-like woman who I guessed to be in her fifties, swung open the door. She was wearing a purple velvet kaftan and her hair was wrapped dramatically in an orange turban. She looked incredibly glamorous with her hooped earrings and thick black Cleopatra-style eyeliner. She looked deep into my eyes for an uncomfortable length of time and then swooped me into a tight embrace, gripping me lovingly against her breast.

"Welcome and love to you, my dear." Her voice was soft and gentle but her vice-like grip was disabling me. I wheezed into her cleavage for what seemed an age and then she dropped me abruptly and swept into her temple.

"Come, come, my love, be at home, you are with the angels now," she said.

I pulled off my boots and coat. I felt hot, sweaty and awkward, but full of hope. This had to work. My chest was sore and my nose and eyes were streaming. I felt a fever coming on and was desperate to feel some relief as I couldn't face another chest infection. I was still on a course of homeopathic remedies and was determined not to take any more antibiotics until I'd given them a chance.

"Lie down, dear." Stargazer stepped back and presented her couch with a dramatic gesture, as if it was the emperor's throne.

I faltered. 'Erm, I can't really lie down right now, my chest is too tight and it makes it worse, I..."

"Wait!" She held up her hand, stopping me mid sentence and closed her eyes. "I am sensing a heavy heart and a need to breathe, you are so burdened with grief."

I burst into tears. I felt really vulnerable and her words hit hard.

"I need to take my inhaler and wait a few minutes, then I can lie down," I whispered. I felt silly for crying and anxious to get on with the session. I pulled my inhaler out of my pocket and sucked in hard. It stung my chest, as it always did when an infection was brewing.

Stargazer stayed stock still with her eyes shut. "It's your inner child, she is desperate for attention, you are disabled with sadness."

I wasn't quite sure what she meant. I agreed that life had been a struggle lately, but I didn't think my life had been bad enough for me to be disabled with sadness. Maybe she was picking up on a memory I had blocked out.

"Do you know the event I am talking about? Can you bring yourself to speak of it?" she asked me gently. As she walked over to me and took my hands, she stared deep into my eyes again.

"Not really. I mean, I can't bring anything to mind at the moment." I tried to hold her gaze but I felt my nose starting to run and tried to pull my hand out of her grip so I could wipe it.

"Allow yourself to absorb the love in my hands." She smiled dreamily at me and it felt too mundane to mention my snotty nose, so I smiled back and tried to make my eyes look as deep and meaningful as hers.

"You can't remember because this is not of this lifetime. A past life is haunting you and we will clear it. In fact, there are many past lives haunting you and we will clear all of them."

She let go of my hand and I was relieved to get a tissue to my nose at last. *Past life? Wow*, I thought. I certainly believed in past lives and I'd toyed with the idea of wanting to know who I had been before. Now, it looked like I was about to find out.

Stargazer drifted over to a throne-like chair and announced that she would tune in until I was ready to lie down. I took the opportunity to take in the room. It was small and overcrowded with crystals, candles, statues of Buddha's, angels and other deities, framed pictures of saintly-looking men and women, angel cards and silk flowers. It was beautiful and overdone. There was a two-bar electric fire in the corner keeping the room at a comfortable temperature.

I walked over to the couch and wiped my nose hopefully for the last time before lying down. Stargazer came and stood over me and spent a long time placing crystals on my body. I realized then that I needed to pee, but decided not to disturb her as she looked deep in trance, so I closed my eyes and tried to go with it, but I felt uncomfortable. Stargazer started to chant, and put her hands over my eyes. Her hands were clammy and her pressure was too heavy. I felt irritated. I badly wanted a miracle, I wanted to experience something amazing, meet God, be shown the secrets of the universe and come out of this session healed and whole.

She moved her hands to my chest and I felt tearful again. Great, something was happening! I was about to release my grief and the cause of my ill health! I started to breathe quickly and heavily, trying to help the process of release. I cried a bit and then my nose started to run again and my bladder got my attention so I gave up on trying to force a spontaneous remission and just lay there feeling pissed off.

Stargazer began to talk. She told me of a past life where I was crushed by a great tree, another where I was shot in the chest, another when I was strangled… By the time she got to the fifth gruesome death, I had lost the will to live and had almost lost control over my bladder! She was in mid flow, telling of a violent stabbing, when I blurted out that I had to go to the toilet. She stopped abruptly, tutted and removed the crystals from my body and I scuttled off the couch and ran out of the room and into the toilet. *Relief at last*! I giggled to myself. I guess you do get what you ask for.

The rest of the session was uneventful. Thankfully, Stargazer had channelled all the lives I needed to know about for now, so I just received the rest of the hands-on healing before handing her a cheque for £40 and getting out of there as quickly as possible. I scurried home feeling like an idiot. I was so desperate that I had lost all sense of judgement, and so low in self-esteem that I didn't even have the confidence to stop her obnoxious treatment and get out of there with my bank account intact.

I was fuming on the train on the way home and I decided to stop off at the gym, fuel myself up with Ventolin and run out my frustrations on the treadmill. The whole session with Stargazer had left me feeling resentful and rebellious. I was missing having those times of feeling exhilarated in my body. I loved the physical demands of being a dancer, being pushed to my limit in rehearsals, feeling on the brink of exhaustion and going beyond it. It was a high I never wanted to live without and the only way I knew of reaching that place was to physically force myself.

There is an old saying in Chinese medicine: 'Bless your illness, it's keeping you healthy'. When I first heard it, it made me so mad! Bless it? Bless this horrible asthma that was robbing me of doing the very thing that brought me so much joy? It made me even more determined to force my body to comply. I felt like that on the tube on the way to the gym. Part of me was aware that my body was asking for rest, and not just in physical form. I knew the mental onslaught that I kept inflicting on myself was just as damaging, but I couldn't help myself.

I marched myself through the reception at the gym like an angry parent yanking a child somewhere she didn't want to go. I threw off my coat and sweatshirt and plunged into my bag for my inhaler, and it wasn't there. It must have fallen out somewhere between Stargazer's and the gym. I was furious. I desperately needed to move, to run, to do something and I would never dare to risk it without my inhaler. I sat in the changing room with my back against the lockers and stared at the wall for what seemed like an age. Eventually, I realised I was staring at the class timetable. Yoga was starting in fifteen minutes. I had never tried yoga as I felt it wouldn't push me enough; however, I was here and ready for action and anything more energetic than yoga would probably put my life in danger. So it was with that attitude that I flounced upstairs to reception and paid for my first yoga class.

I was still intensely irritated by everything that had happened that day and I felt exasperated when I walked into the studio. I rolled my eyes at the sight of everyone lying down quietly on their mats. What way was this to begin a class? No pumping music in the background, getting the adrenalin up, coaxing the body into a rhythm. I lay down and let out a resistant sigh, thinking *six bloody quid to lie on a mat!* I didn't listen to a word the teacher was saying as she talked us through a relaxation exercise, I just wanted to get on with the stretching. Little did I know then that I was about to experience a completely new way of being in my body.

I don't know if it was exhaustion or the deliberate and slow instruction that I finally gave way to, but it wasn't long before I felt myself relax and drop into the gentle guidance coming from the teacher. And, as we were working gently in a pose called Warrior, I noticed a real strength arising from deep inside my structure. Of course I had felt strength in my body before, but not like this. I was fascinated and my internal chatter dropped away as my curiosity deepened with each posture. At the end of the class, I was lulled into a state of relaxation that I had never experienced before. It wasn't the usual buzz and floppiness that I enjoyed after a good workout; this was different. It felt more like an unravelling, a deep satisfaction, like my body was saying 'thank you' and showing me its strength in return. I left the studio in a trance. My mind was calm and my body felt happy, comfortable and worked to the core.

It seems my life has had this pattern of taking sudden twists and turns, and this yoga class was no exception. Treadmills and gyms became a thing of the past as I discovered other ways of being in my body. Over the next few years, I learned that there was a way to dance, move and exercise that was highly satisfying and nurturing. My training and career had been centred on competition and performing. It was a totally alien concept to do something just for the sheer joy of it. My whole conditioning was to achieve, push, have a goal and be praised for it. And, although that was satisfying and enjoyable in itself, it wasn't sustainable in any sense of the word, as the highs were sporadic and short-lived and the reliance on someone's approval also meant that slight criticism could knock me off my pedestal in a flash.

As I attended more and more classes of yoga and mindful movement, and studied Wild Goose Qi Gong with Qi Gong Master Michael Tse, a beautiful and graceful form that consists of two sets of sixty-four movements, I became aware of an 'invisible world' – a deeper aspect to life far more alive and real than simply living within the limitations of the dense world of matter. I finally experienced what I had been reading about and shouting about to everyone else!

The more I acknowledged it through experience rather than information, the more life showed me just how much more there was to the physical aspect of living.

It wasn't a linear transition; in fact, it took many years to drop the 'me' that wanted to fix, achieve, control life and rescue the afflicted. My need to rescue was certainly present in many of my relationships. One of my 'projects' was my dad, who was also struggling with his health. This was a situation that brought me some hard and extremely tender messages and led me to meet one of my most dear friends and teachers.

Chapter Eleven

WHEN THE STUDENT
IS READY...

Dad's health had been declining for some time and he kept it hidden from the family. He was in his mid forties, a self-employed builder and running his own home improvements business, but Mum had noticed he was slowing down and taking more and more time off work. Secretly he was suffering, as he struggled with his breathing and found he was unable to cope with work. He had been visiting the doctor for help and it was only when Mum found a drawer full of empty inhalers that he admitted how bad things were getting. Not long after that, emphysema was diagnosed and Dad was eventually forced to give up work.

Dad's decline was incredibly painful for the whole family and we all dealt with it in our own way. My sisters and their families played a more practical role of being there day-to-day and the grandchildren gave Dad the respite he needed from a disease that left him extremely low. It was hard for Mum. She had nursed her own mother in recent years until she had died. Now, she was at a point in her life where the children had all left home but, instead of it being a phase of her life where she and Dad could follow their own interests and enjoy more leisure time, Dad was now housebound and she had to work full time.

As I was in my 'born again' phase and living over two hundred miles away in London, I took on the role of trying to find a cure for him. The more I discovered, the more desperate I was for Dad to try all the strange things I was finding on my path of healing. I was forever calling him to tell him about something he should be doing or taking or eating. Dad was willing to try alternative stuff but found my approach overwhelming. At the time, I believed I was pushing things on him 'for his own good'. It's obvious to me now that I was fulfilling my own need, not his. Recognising when I am projecting has been a big lesson!

Despite my over-enthusiastic approach, Dad and I formed a kind of bond we had never had before. Although I had always adored my Dad and, when my sisters and I were growing up, there was always plenty of rough and tumble when he came home from work and lots of good-humoured banter, it wasn't until he was suffering from emphysema that I really got to know him as a person and had the chance to appreciate his enquiring mind and poetic outlook on life. Like many men of his generation, he had spent most of his time in the company of other men. He worked hard as a builder in the daytime and would enjoy a pint in the evening in the pub. Living in a female-dominated household with my nan, my mum and his three daughters often left him on the periphery of the family.

Although our ill health was something we had in common and although it led us to share some beautiful experiences, I wish I could have the chance again to adopt a more gentle approach and really listen and get to know him, without my fear driving the relationship.

On one of my visits to Manchester, I took Dad along to a demonstration by my Qi Gong teacher, Michael Tse, who taught in London and Manchester. During the demo, he asked for volunteers to come and experience a 'Qi transmission', which involved him sending his energy into us from the opposite side of the room. I stood up and pulled Dad with me to join the other volunteers, who were seating themselves with eyes closed on a row of chairs that had been placed at the end of the room. We sat with our backs to Michael, who stood about twenty feet away from us. I did as I was instructed and waited. I had just had the thought, *this probably won't work and will put Dad off*, when I felt a surge of what I can only describe as power move slowly through me. A spontaneous intake of breath followed and I felt wonderful. I sat still for quite a few minutes afterwards and when I opened my eyes and looked at Dad, I knew he had had a similar experience. His face was flushed and his breathing calm and he sat still, with a look of awe on his face.

When he finally shifted his focus, he looked at me and said, "Bloody hell... Jesus!" and with that, I knew it had been a good experience for him.

We arranged for Michael to come and visit Dad every two weeks and, as well as transmitting his Qi, he also gave Dad daily Qi Gong exercises. It was both wonderful and weird seeing my dad get up and do his Qi Gong and meditate every morning when I was visiting. This was a man who previously had thought broccoli was exotic! It gave Dad hope and, although his health was poor, over the six months of regular practise, it was improving slowly and he looked forward to Michael's visits.

Like most rhythms in life, it was three steps forwards and two steps back and unfortunately it was on a step back that Michael got too busy to be able to continue his visits. It was a blow to Dad, as he believed Michael had given up on him and no amount of talking could help us persuade him that that wasn't the case. Michael Tse was in big demand and his workshops and classes were growing around the country and he was unable to keep up a private clinic.

The next time I visited my family, I was shocked to see how much Dad had deteriorated. He had given up hope, stopped doing his Qi Gong altogether and his spirits were low. We were sitting at the kitchen table together, making stew for tea and he threw his head in his hands in desperation because he was getting out of breath just chopping carrots. It propelled me into finding another healer and, after a bit of searching, I found out about a cancer care clinic in Cheadle that offered hands-on healing for anyone who was ill and I talked Dad into visiting.

Dad was anxious and uncomfortable on the way there. Even though the family were always willing to take him places, his illness was closing him down and he hadn't been out for months. He was also very hesitant to go to a spiritual healing centre. His breathing got worse as we pulled into the car park and it took a long time for him to get out of the car. Eventually, we made it up the steps and walked into a porta-cabin made up of four rooms. In the main room, several people were sitting on chairs with their eyes closed, looking very peaceful, whilst healers stood with their hands gently touching them, their expressions equally serene. It was an unfamiliar environment for Dad and his breath was rasping above the gentle music.

I hoped someone would come and rescue us from standing in the doorway soon. We didn't have to wait long.

"Alright?" A Liverpudlian accent cut across the serene sounds and a big, burly guy about the same age as Dad, with a shaved head and tattooed arms, came towards us. He looked so out of place that Dad and I just gawped at him for a few seconds.

"I'm Ronnie. I'm one of the healers. Come through to the kitchen, I'll make ya a cuppa."

I felt Dad perk up. This was brilliant! Ronnie was just the kind of guy he could relate to, down to earth and friendly and looked like most of the blokes down the pub.

Whilst we were drinking our tea, Dad and Ronnie chatted about football. Dad was enjoying himself. He didn't have company like this any more. It had been years since he had been to the pub, as his illness had driven him indoors and his friends were not the kind to pop round and keep him company. The men he knew met in the pub and mostly kept their problems and feelings to themselves. It was lovely to see Dad enjoying Ronnie's banter. They chatted a while longer, then Ronnie asked Dad if he would like to experience some healing.

"Go on then, I'll give it a go," Dad said, no doubt a bit uncomfortable at the prospect of Ronnie gently laying his hands on him.

I sat back in my chair and watched as Ronnie placed his hands above Dad's head and they both closed their eyes. The next twenty minutes were profoundly beautiful as I witnessed Dad receiving tender, loving care from a man who looked like he would be more at home in a rugby scrum than a healing centre. The atmosphere was angelic and extraordinarily peaceful. Ronnie's big, clumsy hands became soft and light as he moved around Dad's body, sometimes touching him, sometimes hovering above the surface of his skin. I had tears rolling down my cheeks from the sheer feeling of love and care that was filling the space inside this shabby little cabin.

Eventually, Ronnie stepped away and stood watching Dad sitting peacefully with his eyes closed, obviously in a very special place, his breathing slow and easy, a light expression on his face. Dad eventually opened his eyes and looked surprised to see us there, smiling at him. "Bloody hell!" he said, and I knew it had been very special for him.

He and Ronnie chatted for a while longer and this time, the conversation was a little different, as Dad told Ronnie about his experiences of peace during meditation and Ronnie told Dad all about the beings that assisted him when he gave healing. "I've 'ad Jesus in 'ere, Winston Churchill, angels... you name it, they've bin 'ere."

It's a memory that will warm me in my old age.

We were hoping that Dad could see Ronnie regularly, but we learned that he lived quite a long way away and it was only coincidence he was at this healing centre that day. It was a blow, but Ronnie gave us the phone number of a woman who lived in Cheadle Hulme, who did home visits. This is how we came to meet Marlene.

On the morning Marlene was due to visit, Dad was having a bad day. He had been up most of the night gasping for breath and was tired and low. He was anxious about Marlene coming; he didn't like people seeing him so ill and, even though he had really enjoyed meeting Ronnie and still marvelled at how good he had felt even days after the treatment, he was embarrassed about his condition and found it stressful meeting people outside of the family.

I was feeling anxious, too. I was hoping for someone like Ronnie, someone Dad could relate to and feel relaxed with. Somehow, the name Marlene didn't conjure up a walloping big bloke with a loud laugh and hands the size of table tennis bats. If this went well, Marlene could continue to visit and maybe rekindle Dad's hope...

The doorbell rang and I ran to open it. A slim, elegant and well-dressed woman smiled warmly at me. "Hello, I'm Marlene," she said in a well-spoken voice.

I guess it's fair to say that apart from Marlene being about the same age and having kind eyes, she was the polar opposite of Ronnie. I greeted her as warmly as my whirring head would allow and invited her into the front room. I knew Dad would feel awkward and put his posh voice on. When he was running his own business, he would have people phoning up all the time for estimates and we always knew when somebody well-spoken was on the other end of the phone because Dad would suddenly start 'talking posh'. He would over-emphasise his H's and use k's instead of g's. His 'somethinks' and 'nothinks' were a great source of amusement to me and my sisters.

Dad was slumped in his chair puffing and panting and, when he saw Marlene, he sat bolt upright like a naughty schoolboy who had just been caught smoking behind the bike sheds.

"Oh, hhhello, thanks for coming. Do you want a cup of tea or somethink?" he wheezed

"I'll go and make some," I said breezily and went out of the room.

When I came back in, Dad and Marlene were chatting. I could see Dad had relaxed a little although his words were still quite clipped. Marlene had a warm, easy manner and a peaceful air about her that felt kind and safe. They spoke about Dad's experiences of healing so far and when it came time to do the healing session, he seemed quite comfortable.

I sat quietly as Marlene 'tuned in' to Dad. The air went still and the familiar soft, angelic energy filled the room. Dad went into the zone and his body relaxed. A deep meditative state is so indescribable and yet so familiar, I once heard someone say it was like 'coming home'. I watched Dad drop into deeper and deeper levels of peace, all the unimportant worldly stuff falling away, his class, his gender, beliefs, past hurts, present suffering, fears for the future... leaving only peace. A state where healing can easily step in, and miracles can happen, and it was miraculous to witness. Ten minutes before, he was so uncomfortable, his breathing short and raspy, all his insecurities about being uneducated and assumptions about people he considered to have more authority, bringing out his cap-doffing behaviour. Now, he sat breathing easily and deeply, a half smile on his face.

Marlene stepped back after about twenty minutes and Dad sat for at least another fifteen. I envied where he went to in his meditations; his simple nature seemed to allow him to go to depths that I, at that time, only got glimpses of. In those days, although I had moved on significantly from needing to be recognised and successful in the material sense, I was still too desperate for enlightenment. I wanted peace and freedom so badly and the glimpses I had experienced spurred me on to have more. I would often sit and meditate with so many hopes and expectations, wrangling in my busy mind, longing to be able to just switch off and just be, that when I occasionally did slide into 'the zone', that wonderful, still state, my monkey mind would immediately start chattering again, excited about the fact I had stepped into peace for that moment, and jerk me back to my usual state of constant internal commentary.

When Dad opened his eyes, he was so relaxed he didn't even swear.

As Marlene began to visit Dad regularly, his k's soon got dropped from the end of his words and he no longer adjusted his posture when she came in. He looked forward to her visits and really valued her friendship. For me, it was the beginning of one of the most important relationships of my life.

Healing wasn't something that Marlene had done all her life; in fact, it had only been in the last decade that she had discovered her gift.

In the October of 1988, Marlene and her husband, Peter, had booked to go to a talk about 17th century England at the local university. Upon arriving, they discovered it had been cancelled so they decided to go to the only other talk available, which was on Parapsychology. Val Peal, a medium and a healer, presented it and, after thoroughly enjoying her presentation, Peter, who had been feeling unwell, arranged a healing session with Val, which led to regular visits when his health began to improve.

After one particular session, he came home to tell Marlene that he had experienced something that had "taken the biscuit": He went on to explain that Val had used a pendulum to ask questions and get guidance during the healing session. She had called it dowsing. Val had told him that it was something anyone could do, and it was a way of asking for guidance from invisible forces. All that was required was a string or chain with something on the end to give it a bit of weight. The next thing would be to ask a few questions to find out how the pendulum moved when giving a 'yes' or a 'no' answer. This was done by asking a basic question like "is my name…?" and using your real name to find the movement for 'yes', and using a false name to find the movement for 'No'. Once the Yes and No were established, it was a matter of practice and experimenting to perfect the art.

It sparked Marlene's interest and she put a pendulum together and was amazed to find that it did indeed spin in different directions, one indicating a 'Yes' and the opposite way a 'No'. She had been experiencing a lot of aches and discomfort in her legs and was about to take a course of HRT to see if it would help but, seeing as she had stumbled on this new skill, she decided to postpone cashing in the prescription and check via dowsing to see if there were certain foods that were affecting her. The dowsing showed a negative on quite a few things and, after two weeks of cutting those foods out, her legs were completely pain-free.

She was intrigued with what she had experienced and, not long after that, when she was visiting her brother and sister-in-law, she got the chance to dowse in a different way. Yvonne, her sister-in-law, was experiencing some health problems and Marlene offered to dowse to see if they could gain some clarity. As she dowsed over Yvonne's body, Yvonne mentioned that she could feel the same kind of sensation through Marlene's hands as she felt when her husband, Marlene's brother, 'rubbed away' her headaches, which was something about her own brother that Marlene had never known. Marlene's dowsing indicated a problem in Yvonne's kidneys and her doctor later confirmed it when he diagnosed a kidney infection.

The following spring, Marlene and Peter went on a trip to the States and they stayed with friends they had met on a previous holiday. It turned out that these friends were staunch Methodists and, as their house guests, Marlene and Peter joined them when they went to their Sunday Service. As it happened, the whole service was about healing. "You must go out and heal" was the primary message. The next Sunday, they attended the service again and, to Marlene's surprise, it was the same message, "You must go out and heal", and she got a feeling she was meant to be listening!

A few days later, when they were on a trip to the North Rim of the Grand Canyon, Marlene got the chance to follow orders. Peter, who had been very excited about their trip to North Rim to watch the sun go down, was feeling dreadfully ill with a tummy bug on the day they were due to go. Remembering what Yvonne had said about her brother rubbing away headaches and the fact she felt the same sensation from Marlene's hands, she offered to rub Peter's tummy. As she did so, Peter started to shake quite violently and then fell into a deep sleep. Marlene was worried, as she had no idea what to make of this reaction. However, on awakening, Peter was completely better and ready to enjoy the day.

All these experiences opened up a new way of approaching life and its possibilities for both Marlene and Peter. It led Marlene to explore and develop her skills of healing and receiving messages and since then, she has been guided as to how to balance the earth and cosmic life force energies that have a profound effect on our physical, mental and emotional health. Peter learned that he had a particular gift for dowsing and clearing earth energies and became very adept at clearing negative energies from environments, leaving them balanced and cleansed. It's a practice that is still understood and respected in many other cultures.

Over the years, both Marlene and Peter have been a great source of strength, support and wisdom to me, a friendship that I hold very dear.

Chapter Twelve

HAPPY DAYS

Not long after meeting Marlene, Dad had a lung transplant and she played a key role in his preparation during the weeks prior to the operation. Through a combination of hands-on and distant healing and flower remedies, she worked on balancing his energies and getting him into a positive mind-set. There were different opinions in the family towards this alternative approach – not everyone understood or believed in 'healing' – but it was clear to everyone that something was working and making a big difference to Dad, and so it was accepted and supported.

When Dad went into hospital, Marlene's husband, Peter, cleared and healed the energies in the hospital ward and the operating theatre. It's an unfamiliar thing in our culture and yet, in others, it is as important to clear the energy of illness, death and thought forms of fear, sadness and grief in a building, as it is to keep it physically clean and germ-free.

On the day Dad went down to the operating theatre, the medical team were very doubtful that he would make it through the operation, as his lungs were so damaged from years of heavy smoking and, as a builder, knocking out chimneybreasts containing asbestos. Although he had a strong spirit and a positive mind, his body was weak. It would be a long operation and we were advised to go home until Dad was out of theatre.

It was an emotional day. Mum, my sisters Kaye and Max and I spent the time at Mum and Dad's house and we were all on tenterhooks. We eventually got the call that the operation had been a success, and the next crucial stage would be taking Dad off the respirator. That would be the moment when his body would either accept his new lung and allow him to breathe on his own, or reject it, which meant we would lose him. We were told to stay put as Dad was in intensive care and still not allowed visitors.

A few hours later, we decided to go up to the hospital and wait there; it was agonising sitting around, jumping out of our skins every time the phone rang. It would be a while before they attempted taking Dad off the respirator, but at least we would be close by.

As we were leaving, though, the phone rang with surprising and wonderful news. It was the hospital informing us that Dad was off the respirator and ready for visitors. The nurse also told us that although people were normally shocked and drowsy for some time after coming off a respirator, Dad had immediately announced that he was starving and asked if he could have bacon and eggs! It was such a special moment of delight and relief for us. I called Marlene with the news and arranged to meet her at the hospital.

Dad was in a private room and, as we walked up the corridor towards it, the first thing I saw was his foot sticking out of the covers, tapping along to a lively song he was listening to on his headphones. I walked through the doorway and saw the rest of him lying on his bed, eyes closed, smiling away and thoroughly enjoying the music. My heart swelled. It had been a long time since any of us had seen him looking so comfortable and carefree. He greeted us in such a light-hearted way – his breathing seemed clear and it was easy for him to talk and he looked bright and rested – it was as if he had just got back from a long holiday, rather than having just spent the day undergoing major surgery.

A nurse was bustling around the room. She greeted us with a bright smile and Dad introduced her as if she was an old friend. Then, to the surprise of all of us, he said to the nurse, "Oh and this is Marlene, the healer I was telling you about." We hadn't expected Dad to be so open about having a healer. I also noticed he had his rescue remedy and crystals on his bedside table.

We chatted for a while and then, when Marlene offered him some healing, he accepted and we all pushed our chairs back to make some room around the bed and the nurse respectfully went out of the room. Marlene stood with her hands over Dad and began her healing session. A hushed stillness came over the room. Even the noise of the machines seemed to go quiet. Mum, Kaye, Maxine and I sat still and watched. Marlene worked just above Dad's body. Sometimes her hands shook quite violently, sometimes they were very still. The atmosphere of peace built up in the room and, by the time Marlene stepped away, Dad was lying completely still, more peaceful than I had ever seen him look. In fact, he was so still that, for a fleeting moment, I panicked and my eyes flew to the monitor his heart was wired up to. With relief, I saw the jagged line indicating his heartbeat and once again became aware of the welcome intermittent bleep.

The nurse breezed back in at this moment and stopped short in the doorway as if something had physically stopped her. Just then, Dad made a sound like someone being jolted awake. He kept his eyes closed, burst into tears and just sobbed and sobbed.

I had only ever seen my dad cry twice before. The first time was when I was eleven years old and his brother-in-law, our uncle David, died of a brain tumour. He was sitting at the kitchen table after the tragic news when he suddenly let out a loud sob. He stood up immediately, tipping his chair over with the suddenness of his movement and walked out of the room, hiding his face. The only other time I saw him with tears in his eyes was when I was nineteen and he and Mum took me to the airport when I was leaving home to work in Italy. I went through the barrier and looked back, catching Mum in floods of tears and Dad all choked up. Just like the time when he'd cried about Uncle Dave, he hid his face by turning and walking away.

In his hospital bed after the healing session, Dad sat unashamedly sobbing, his face contorted and soaking wet, nose running, taking in massive gulps of air for what seemed like an age as he just let it all out. For him to do such a thing in front of a room full of women would have been, at one time, unthinkable to him. It was wonderful to watch his release; in fact, we all joined in, even the nurse! In Chinese medicine, the lungs house the emotion of grief and, although I could never prove this, I knew we were witnessing the root cause of his emphysema being released, as he let go of whatever had been constricting and eating away at his lungs for decades. When the sobbing finally subsided, Dad told us how "bloody marvellous" the healing session had felt, and the reason he had kept his eyes shut for so long was because he was convinced that he had been picked up by a group of people and then left floating above the bed and he had been too scared to open his eyes in case it was true!

Seeing Dad in tears became quite normal over the next few weeks. He cried freely whenever somebody gave him a get-well card, when his grandchildren visited, when someone else on his ward was suffering. He was full of compassion and gratitude. He also made heartfelt connections with the other men on the ward and became a source of inspiration to other patients. Dad being in touch with his feelings and allowing them to be seen, was new to all of us. Although he was always warm and jovial, emotions made him uncomfortable and he usually let Mum deal with that kind of stuff. However, after he came out of hospital, he would be the first to comfort someone in trouble, always ready to listen to someone's problems and help where he could.

Dad's medical team were fantastic and incredibly supportive. They seemed to enjoy the success of the operation and the effect it had had on our newborn Dad as much as we did. His surgeon was a very respectful and open man, who talked a lot about the power of the mind and positive thinking. He once told Dad that there had been times when they had lost somebody on the operating table who should have sailed through. He believed it was the mind-set of the person that made the difference between life and death. Although the surgeon and the consultants didn't make any direct comments about the healing, they gave space for it and, in an indirect way, acknowledged that it played a part in his rapid recovery, at which they were openly amazed. Apparently, none of them had expected Dad to survive the operation; when they opened him up, his lung had almost jumped out at them, it was so badly damaged and deflated. They expected that, if he recovered at all, it would be a very long and slow process. Him coming off the respirator and asking for bacon and eggs was the first surprise, and they kept coming!

In fact, they told us that his recovery, including the healing sessions he had, had been talked about at a recent conference, and the nurses noted his healing sessions in his records. Dad became the 'positive-thinking man'. However, as is the protocol of defensive medicine, they kept warning him about his high spirits and telling him to be aware that he could come down with a bump, which can be common post-surgery. It was a prediction that, thankfully, never manifested.

There were a few other interesting things that occurred around Dad being in hospital. As he was moved from the operating theatre, to intensive care, then onto a private room and eventually a ward, Peter, Marlene's husband, kept clearing the spaces he moved into. The private room was usually a place that people stayed in, sometimes for weeks, as they recovered from major operations. We kept hearing comments from the nurses about how quickly people were recovering and moving onto the wards and then home. One man who had been in hospital for over a year, went in the private room after Dad, after suffering yet another complication and, after only three weeks, returned home.

It is not acknowledged in our modern day thinking that places have an energy. Although we all talk about 'atmosphere' and 'feelings' that buildings have, we rarely acknowledge that experiences, thought forms and old energy can hang around in our buildings and affect us if they are not cleared. Our attitude is not shared by many cultures of the world. In Bali, for example, energetic space clearing is just as important as cleaning the dust away. In fact, they have daily purification rituals in order to keep their buildings healthy, as well as intermittent elaborate rituals to keep their island healthy.

Our environment affects our health and vitality as well as our ability to heal and move on. Everyone knows how it feels to walk into a room after two people have had an argument. Clearing the energetic imprint of the argument in other cultures is as important as clearing up the disagreement. In hospitals around the world, energetic space clearing is as common as changing the sheets. I believe that the space-clearing Peter did, along with the healing he received from Marlene, had a profound effect on Dad's recovery and the recovery of the other patients who were in the immediate environment.

Dad was soon back home and we all have our own special memories of watching him dive into his life with gusto. The day after he came home from hospital, I walked around the block with him to get a newspaper. He hadn't done that for at least seven years and it was like taking a toddler on his first walk. He stopped in amazement at every little thing he saw. Shoots popping up on the borders of a garden, new paving on a neighbour's pathway, he noticed every minute change in the neighbourhood with childlike wonder.

Dad kept saying he had been given "a second bite of the cherry" and, for the next sixteen months before his death, he lived his life to the full. He was so grateful to be alive and every morning in his meditation he thanked the medical team, Marlene and Peter and everyone who had sent him or given him healing, or simply wished him well. He also thanked the donor of his lung and her family.

One time, after we had walked around our local water park, as he was getting into the passenger seat of the car he stopped, turned and, in a spontaneous moment of appreciation, he shook his fists at the sky and shouted, "THANK YOU, LOVE!" at the top of his voice, with so much passion. He was addressing his donor, who had been a young woman in her thirties. He was just so grateful to her that he was alive and well.

As my brother-in-law Paul said at his funeral, "Although Dave didn't go skydiving or parachuting, he did live his life to the full. He took his second chance seriously. He made sure his family knew how much he loved them by being thoughtful and demonstrative. He also took time to listen to others' worries and share his experiences in order to help. He relished his 'second bite of the cherry' and simply demonstrated that it is available to all of us, just as soon as we want to take it."

Chapter Thirteen

BIG DECISIONS

Stories of transplant patients taking on certain characteristics or memories even skills that previously belonged to their donors are well documented. Food cravings and changes of tastes in music as well as memories, appear to have been transplanted along with the organ.

Having read these stories, it was no surprise to me when, soon after his lung transplant, Marlene channelled a message that informed her that it was important that she cut the ties with Dad's donor. This would allow the donor to be free and to move on in spirit and Dad would be able to accept his new lung as his own. After asking Dad's permission, which he readily agreed to, Marlene cut the ties in the way she would perform an absent healing session.

For a year, Dad continued to go from strength to strength and then things took a strange turn; his body started rejecting the steroids. He was beginning to get breathless again. According to allopathic medicine, in order for the body to accept a foreign organ the immune system needs to be suppressed by use of steroids. A strong immune system would immediately reject the transplanted organ, which would inevitably result in death.

This is one of the major downsides of a transplant operation, as the side effects of steroids can be strong and unpleasant, including thinning of the skin and bloating. Dad was already on the minimum dose needed and his consultant was concerned. Soon after the complications started, Marlene contacted Dad as she had channelled another message regarding his lung: a message stating that he no longer needed to take steroids. The ties with the donor had been severed and therefore his body could now accept the lung as his own. She was told that the steroids would eventually start making his body react as if it was overdosing on the medication, if he continued to take them.

Obviously it was a huge decision for Dad to make. Could he really place his trust in Marlene's message and risk his body rejecting his new lung? Then a message came via a completely different route: Dad turned on the TV one evening and there happened to be a programme on about four people who had had different kinds of organ transplants. All of them had thrown away their steroids after experiencing severe side affects and, contrary to medical understanding, they had lived. One woman had done so after a liver transplant as she found her steroids made her violent towards her son. She was so afraid of harming him that one day, she just threw her prescribed drugs away and took a chance. The other people had similar stories. It was too synchronistic to see this programme on top of Marlene's message and ignore it, so Dad booked an appointment with his consultant. He wanted to try and give up his steroids.

The consultation didn't go as he had hoped. The consultant, who had been quite supportive of Dad's complementary approach, told Dad under no circumstances could he stop taking his medication. Dad persevered, asking if he could come into hospital and do it under close observation. I think the consultant panicked at this point; this was too far out of his understanding and training and he told Dad he would die if he came off steroids and that he should also stop taking his flower remedies and having healing sessions.

This was such a blow. After witnessing such a beautiful blend of allopathic medicine and all its skill and knowledge working alongside the power of natural medicine and healing, it was so obvious that both aspects were equally important and complimented each other beautifully. The medical industry is a piece of the pie, and a very important piece, but it isn't the whole pie. In fact, it is the only medical system that does not acknowledge that there is a greater intelligence that is vital to the healing process. Cases like Dad's and the ones on the television programme are considered 'coincidences'; they don't fit into our scientific model and therefore can't be measured and proven. Instead, they are simply rejected.

Dad was completely deflated when he came home and was far too scared to risk stopping his medication. He was also upset that he had offended his medical team, as he was so grateful for what they had done and had promised faithfully to keep up his medication. Everyone was disappointed that Dad couldn't at least try to come off the medication. We were also frightened by the consultant's prediction of the outcome should he attempt to, so we backed his decision. I did so reluctantly, as I totally trusted Marlene's work and wished he would take a chance. I was happy, however, that he decided to still keep up his complimentary approach and continue with his Qi Gong, meditation, healing and flower remedies.

It wasn't long before things got complicated. Dad became very bloated and his skin was so thin he bled easily. It was clear his body was struggling with the steroids. After a while, his old lung started to push against the new one and he had to go back into hospital so his old lung could be operated on.

Chapter Fourteen

GOODBYE, DAD

Dad was chirpy enough when he came round from his operation, which was considered a success. He was happy to see the nurses and doctors that he considered his 'old friends' and was due to return home in a week's time. After a few days of visiting, I felt it was okay for me to go back to London. I kissed Dad goodbye and left his bedside. As I was walking out of the ward, I looked round and saw him through the round window of the door as it was closing behind me. He was smiling and waving at me and I pushed away a strange feeling we were waving to each other for the last time. I was right.

I got the call a day later. Dad's health had taken a sudden turn for the worse, his kidneys had packed up and he was on a dialysis machine in intensive care. I rushed back to Manchester and the rest of the week was a blur.

Dad was unconscious and we took shifts in sitting by his bed. Maxine had gone on holiday with her family the day after the operation. It had been booked for a while and he had insisted she still went ahead with it when his date for the operation came through. After the success of his transplant, we were all expecting him to sail through. We called her to let her know the turn of events and she was in the process of getting return flights for the family. The rest of us swapped shifts so someone was always with Dad.

My emotions swung, as did everyone else's, from being completely positive that Dad was going to make it through, to complete despair that we may lose him. I called Marlene every day and she and Peter were a constant source of support. I did as much healing as I could whilst I was by his bedside, anything I could remember; sound healing, laying of hands, visualization, prayer... I also read to him about Hawaii because, in one of his moments of spontaneity, he had booked a holiday for him and Mum.

They were due to go there in two months' time and had both been really looking forward to it. I figured if I kept talking about it to him, it would give him some strength to pull through. Even though he was unconscious, I knew he could still hear. We never stop hearing, no matter how deeply unconscious we are. There are many accounts of people recalling what had been said to them whilst they where in comas or being operated on. There is an anecdote of a young boy who had his tonsils out. After the operation, he didn't heal and this puzzled his doctors, who had fully expected a speedy recovery and couldn't see any reason why the boy wasn't getting well. It was only when a nurse recalled that during the operation there was a conversation about another patient and how they probably would not heal, that the surgeon, who, thankfully, was open-minded and believed strongly in the power of suggestion, concluded that the boy, although unconscious at the time, had understood them to be talking about him and was therefore fulfilling the prophecy.

They decided to do a mock operation and put the child to sleep for a few moments, after telling him that they just needed to do a simple procedure to help him heal. Once he was unconscious, they talked over him, saying how this would certainly be a success now and he would heal quickly. Sure enough, the boy made a speedy recovery.

Whilst Dad was in intensive care, we would be called into the consultant's office intermittently, so they could keep us updated on how things were going. It was never good news and it was made pretty clear to us that they didn't think he had much chance of survival. One day, during one of these meetings, the consultant asked us if Dad had ever stopped taking his steroids. We reassured him that that wasn't the case, because Dad had been far too scared to come off them after being told he would die.

It was then the consultant said, "You see, at the moment your father is reacting as if he has had an overdose, which is exactly what would have happened if he had stopped taking his steroids."

Marlene's words rang in my ears: "The message I am getting is that if your dad continues to take the steroids, his body will react like it has overdosed. He no longer needs the steroids, as the ties have been cut so the lung no longer belongs to the donor."

I couldn't believe it! I felt stunned and excited at the same time. What if we could get Dad off the steroids now? Would he recover? I was convinced he would. The consultant finished by saying he didn't think Dad had much time left.

Kaye broke down in tears and sat with her head in her hands, sobbing. It was the first time I had seen her give up and it scared me. Mum just looked numb and terrified. I did my usual and tried to come up with something to save the day. I reminded them about what Marlene had said and we agreed to ask them to take Dad off the steroids. We called the consultant back into the office and asked him to honour Dad's request to come off the steroids. To our amazement and relief, he agreed.

This was a blessing and an omen as, although it was what we wanted in order for Dad to have a chance to survive, the fact that the consultant was willing to agree to the request meant that he had lost hope that Dad would live and he was simply honouring a dying man's wish. Kaye went to see Dad and then went home. I think she knew then that he was going to die; she had told me before that she didn't want to be there if he passed away. When she said she wasn't going to come back that night, I knew she was expecting him to go. Maxine was still trying to sort out her flights. It must have been unbearable for her.

Mum and I spent the night at Dad's bedside. Although I was scared about how I would react if the time came, I really wanted be with him if he passed over. I was afraid I might scream and try and hold him back, as in the past, whenever the consultants had given us bad news in that tiny office, I would feel my legs go to jelly and a scream catch in my throat. I swore to myself that I wouldn't scream if Dad started to pass. I wanted to help him go peacefully. Mum and I sat and talked to him, did hands-on healing together, dozed, looked bewildered, then hopeful, then scared. She sat in the comfy armchair by his head and I would sit at his feet and every now and then we would swap places. It was a long night. I kept watching the machine that kept his heart beating and willing it to keep going and visualizing him sitting up and asking for bacon and eggs and the consultants rushing in incredulous about the fact he had woken completely healed.

It was 4.45am when I noticed the daylight seeping through the blinds. I felt a surge of happiness. Dad had made it into another day. I was sitting at the bottom of the bed holding his feet, my head resting on the bed and Mum was asleep holding his hand. She looked frail and vulnerable and I wished I could take her pain away. I wondered at the memories she was having. The day they met, the young love they'd shared, creating a home and raising kids, the rows, the regrets, the frustrations and pain, the love and the good times, all interwoven in the story they had created together.

I dozed off again. A short time after, I felt something urging me out of my seat, a gentle but forceful push and I was at Dad's side before I realised where I was. Mum had also stirred from her sleep and was standing up next to him. We knew he was leaving and it was time to say goodbye and I believe he had woken us so we could do just that. I felt a huge presence behind me, the presence that had urged me out of my chair. It was a soft gold light and I felt totally safe. No danger of screaming or crying or going to pieces. I felt calm and clear.

"It's okay, Dad," I said, "we will all be okay. Off you go, there's nothing to fear." It felt so natural. I kept talking and Mum stroked his head.

He had been on a respirator that had been breathing for him for the past week but at the moment of his death, his body did three short, sharp in-breaths on its own and then shuddered. It was then that I saw all the life drain out of his face as his soul left his body. He was gone.

Neither Mum nor I wanted to linger after that. He wasn't there any more. There was just the empty shell that was once filled with Dad's spirit. I felt calm and complete; there was nothing left to say, nothing more to do. I knew Dad was safe and on the next part of his journey. Mum looked vulnerable and lost and for once, I didn't even try and put anything right. It was time to grieve.

Would Dad still be alive if he had trusted and thrown away his steroids a few months earlier? I believe the answer is yes. I also respect the reaction of the consultant and Dad's decision not to take the risk. We all have our choices to make in life and we will all leave our bodies behind at some point and maybe, for Dad, that was the perfect moment to move on.

We buried Dad a week later on his 58th birthday. It was the perfect date on which to celebrate his life.

Chapter Fifteen

THE FOG LIFTS

Although the experiences around Dad's illness and death were profound and there were some unforgettable experiences of life in all its raw and tender beauty, after his death, I found it hard to integrate them and it wasn't long before that trust and connection I had experienced so powerfully, dwindled. I had watched Dad enjoy a deep connection to life, not because he had achieved anything, but because he simply woke up to everything that he already had and began to live his life in gratitude, the most rewarding and fulfilling way to live.

I was determined to hold on to that after his death but, although I had witnessed it, it wasn't my experience and as much as I wanted to feel that sense of gratitude and that life was enough just as it was, it wasn't long before I was back in the swing of things, trying to use what I had learned so far to change all the things I didn't want in my life; my bad health, living from hand to mouth financially, my career, which seemed to have been swallowed up by aerobics and body conditioning classes and my relationships, which so far had been either short-lived and non-committal, or long, complicated, controlling and needy.

Most of all, I wanted to get rid of this constant feeling of anxiety that was the backdrop to my emotional state. At times, it escalated to a feeling of panic and desperation, but mostly it was there as a low-grade buzz. It sapped the joy out of my world and drove me to try and gain more control over my life and change it. Although I had made some pretty big changes already and had had some profound experiences, the voice of fear was still loud and clouding my judgement. It was difficult to really trust and let go of trying too hard.

Things seemed to be looking up when I was offered a job at the Edinburgh Fringe Festival, dancing and reciting poetry in a children's show. It meant getting away from my life for three weeks and hopefully would be the start of a run of good luck. I enjoyed being part of a performance again. It meant working with new people and being creative and I loved being in Brighton every day, which is where the rehearsals were based. It felt light and fresh and going back to London in the evenings to teach my classes was a chore. I needed them and resented them, but it still came as an almighty shock one day when, out of the blue, I got sacked!

I sat with the class co-ordinator, who had called me to a meeting. She gave me the news and my immediate feeling was shame. I was being sacked from one of the most prestigious clubs in London because a member had complained about my attitude. I knew I deserved it. There was no calling the card of unfair dismissal. It was a sought-after job and instructors at the top of their field worked hard here to maintain their reputation, constantly keeping up with the new fitness fads, the latest outfits and new information. There was no room for someone like me, who was there just so I could pay my bills.

I sat there speechless, with tears in my eyes and it took about ten seconds before the feeling of shame subsided and excitement rose in the pit of my stomach. It was a strange, 'Oh no, oh yes' experience. This was what I really wanted. Freedom! I had no idea what I was going to do but I knew it was time for change and I needed some space in my life in order to do it. I stood up and walked out of the club for the last time with my head in the air and went home to pack for the Edinburgh Festival.

After three fun-filled weeks performing and partying, I came back ready to change my life. I still had no idea how, but I could feel change in the air and determination in my bones and I was going to move a mountain. In order to keep myself focused, I bought a book I had heard about, called *The Artist's Way: A Course in Discovering and Recovering Your Creative Self*, by Julia Cameron. It was a twelve week course that promised to dissolve barriers, rediscover my talents, unleash my creativity and put me on the path to fulfilling my dreams.

Along with weekly exercises that focused on different areas of life, the course also assigned the task of filling three pages with free -flow writing every morning. No thinking or planning, just writing whatever came to mind. The instruction was not to read back anything until week eight. I was diligent about the course. It gave me an anchor as I ran around like a headless chicken, trying to earn enough to support myself and find a new life.

I had been looking forward to reading back my pages and I put a full day aside to do so as week eight approached. The instruction was to read them and highlight anything that may be of value. For instance, any negative thoughts that kept recurring, stuff I may be moaning about and not doing anything to change, or any dreams I had that were clearly ready to move off the page and into action.

The day before the start of week eight, I had had a particularly bad day. I had failed an audition and had my purse pinched on the tube on the way home. I had spent the evening guzzling a bottle of wine on my own, as my housemate of the time was in his room with a new girlfriend. I went to bed full of angst and misery, with a blocked nose and a sore chest, convinced that none of this New Age crap was working.

I woke up unable to move. My body ached all over, my head felt like someone had stuffed it with cotton wool and I felt sick and shaky. I breathed in and heard my lungs rasping and wheezing. How I hated that sound! With a sinking heart, it dawned on me that it was still the dead of night. I figured I had only slept for a short while – half an hour, an hour if I was lucky. That awful noise of my lungs rasping as they struggled to draw breath had woken me like a thousand ghostly screams vying for my attention.

I lay still, trying to elongate the pause between my out-breath and the next in-breath, which was the only time I felt some relief. When I could hold it no longer, I would tense myself with my in-breath; as my lungs burned with a heavy sadness, the out-breath wailed relentlessly and made me want to cry and scream with anger. None of this was unfamiliar. It was yet another chest infection which meant either I had to go and get antibiotics, or leave it to run its course, which meant running the risk of it getting worse and me having to have intravenous steroids and a short stay in hospital. I wanted to stay off drugs, to give my body a chance to get stronger... to find a cure rather than constantly silencing the symptoms. Hours later, I lay immobile and watched the first light change the room from a blue-black to a cold grey. The light slowly revealed the outline of my bedside table and on it sat my morning pages.

I reached over and opened the metal ring-bound book that had become the place to pour out my thoughts each day. I had dutifully written every morning for eight weeks and followed the instructions of just writing, without thinking, censoring or considering anything. As I read back those thoughts, I came face to face with myself. Although they were my words in my writing, it was like reading someone else's diary. Was this lost, frightened, angry person really me? Had I really grown this unhappy and discontented with life? At thirty-two years of age, I was drinking too much and thinking too much and, although I had all the theory, a fair amount of practice and had had some profound experiences, I was still running around like a lunatic hoping to improve my life. In spite of all my preaching about thinking positive thoughts, it was fear that snapped at my heels and motivated me from morning 'til night.

It was a painful morning and I don't know whether it was the state of my health or that over the last few years of experimenting, something had finally shifted, but that morning I took a really good, honest look at myself and, instead of judging, scolding and jumping into action, I found some compassion. For once, I just read and listened to what I had been saying, and it felt good to be heard by the only person who could really make the difference.

It was mid afternoon by the time I got out of bed and I found that my chest felt easier and was no longer sore. I had never recovered that quickly before. Nothing can be more powerful than personal experience and that day, as I experienced my physical symptoms subsiding when I was finally kind and supportive of myself, I realised just how much of an impact my emotions and state of mind were having on my health. It was the start of having peace at the top of my agenda, and entering the mystery of life rather than resisting it. It was time to work from the inside out and view life as magical and full of possibility.

Chapter Sixteen

ALL CHANGE

In order to give myself some space, I decided to stop auditioning and I applied for unemployment benefit for the first time since I started work. I also decided to move to Brighton where I didn't know anybody and live alone for the first time in my life. I started to visualise the kind of place I wanted to live in, a real haven, a place where I could rest and make a transition; into what, I had no idea, but I knew it was important to make the first steps and create a new environment.

I turned to Marlene for long-distance healing, which made a huge difference to my health, and I often phoned her to check my decisions with her dowsing. I really appreciated the way she always handed things back to me when I got too needy. She would help but not hinder by doing it for me, or simply tell me what to do. She always encouraged me to make the final decision and trust my intuition. It was during this time our relationship developed into the friendship that I treasure today. Experiencing the benefits of her healing and the accuracy of her dowsing helped me to reconnect with the invisible world I had experienced through Yoga, Qi

Gong and meditation and I rekindled my practice, this time cultivating my own way of connecting and seeking guidance with this higher intelligence, a spirit that I call God, but which has nothing to do with manmade religion or dogma; a life force that is given to us freely and unconditionally, ever present and ever loving, both inside and outside of us.

I love the story of the three angels who met at the beginning of the world to decide where they should hide God. "In the bottom of the ocean," said the first angel. "On the top of the highest mountain," said the second. In the end, they decided on the third angel's suggestion, which was, "Let's hide God deep inside of each person, because that will be the last place they will look."

In order to prepare for my big move from London to Brighton and a new me, I cleared bags and bags of clutter that I had accumulated since living in London, and every evening I sat and visualised exactly the kind of place I wanted to move into. A spacious and light one-bedroom flat, with sea views and a balcony. I was relying on housing benefit, so when I made my first house-hunting visit to Brighton after two weeks of visualising, I went straight to the housing office. I sat in the waiting room with a large group of other people in need of homes, some drinking out of cans of beer, others flicking through papers that offered jobs available, a few buried in books or just staring out of the window. Most looked more desperate than I did to find a home and my confidence in my plan to state exactly what I wanted and not take second best, was starting to look at best a bit silly and at worst downright ridiculous. When my name was called, I took a deep breath and strode up to the desk.

When the woman asked how she could help, I did something that Marlene had told me about. I imagined putting a bunch of pink roses in her head and sent her lots of good energy as I smiled warmly at her and described what I was looking for. Her gaze didn't waver and she showed no surprise or scorn. Instead, she picked up a sheet of paper and told me they had a one-bedroom flat that had come in that morning and the landlord was happy to deal with housing benefit and only wanted a month's rent as a deposit and I could probably view it that morning. Wow, thank you, Marlene! That certainly seemed to get me over the first hurdle! Not only was I not laughed out of the office, but I had an address in my hand and was on my way to my first viewing.

"Norfolk Square," I muttered to myself as I turned off the main high street and watched out for the street sign. "Ah, there it is." I turned into the street and halfway down, I could see a man waiting by the entrance to some flats. Steve introduced himself and we walked up the stairs to a door of an Edwardian building that was set slightly back from the end of the corner of the road that promised sea views. Never mind, I told myself. It was still close to the sea, even if I couldn't see it from the flat.

Flat 4 opened up into a dark hallway and immediately on the left was a small bedroom that looked out onto the fire escape. Next to the bedroom, halfway down the corridor, was a small bathroom with a tiny window that let in some light from the living room. Despite it falling short of my visualisation, it felt quite nice; it was clean and had a cosy, homely energy. I followed Steve as he continued down the corridor and gasped as we stepped into a beautiful living room. It was large, with a high ceiling, and light flooded in through the huge windows on the far side of the room. I walked over to look out of them onto the street below and realised we were right on the corner of the building and were looking out down the road to the sea.

There was no balcony, but when Steve pushed up the lower half of the ceiling to floor sash-window, it was as near as dammit! It felt as if the whole wall had opened up and looking down through the gaping hole onto the road below made me feel dizzy with excitement. I felt a thrill rush down my spine. I wasn't alone, my unseen friends had been listening to me.

"I'll take it," I said through a tight throat, resisting the urge to throw my arms around Steve and shriek that I had manifested this. I spent the rest of the day on a complete high, signed the papers and skipped back to London. I had another six weeks to wait for everything to go through, but I had my moving-in date and I had paid my deposit. I was ready to embrace change.

Chapter Seventeen

SMALL, DARK AND FAMILIAR

I loved Brighton. It was vibrant, fresh and new. Even though it was a cold, wet March, it was still fantastic to wake up to the sound of seagulls every day and marvel at the ever-changing sea. I loved living on my own. I would often get up in the middle of the night and dance naked around my living room – just because I could. It was such a novelty to put things where I wanted them, make a mess without worrying about annoying someone else and lie in the bath as long as I wanted, without depriving someone else of their birthright to relieve themselves when they needed to.

I had two intentions once I had unpacked. The first was to find a good yoga class, which I soon found only a minute's walk from my flat. The second was to find a drumming course, which, I suspected, was easy in a town saturated with musicians and artists. I got more than I bargained for when I popped into a natural health centre that was offering African Djembe drum classes. The guy informed me there were no places left until the autumn, but he did know of a company called Red Zebra who, amongst other things, taught drumming.

I called them and arranged to meet Mark, who had just started the company with his friend Ollie. We sat and chatted most of the afternoon. Mark was wearing a pair of cut-off jeans and a long baggy t-shirt and he had the habit of throwing his long dreadlocks back whenever he got excited, which was often. He was warm and friendly and full of enthusiasm and I liked him instantly. I learned that he and Ollie had met while drumming on the streets of Brighton, when a large group used to gather every Sunday at the West Pier. They became good friends and had started Red Zebra so they could earn a living doing what they loved. At present, they were doing pretty well for a young company, facilitating drumming and dance classes in schools and special needs centres, as well as taking on the odd corporate job. They were currently recruiting people to work with them as the work was growing and Mark offered me a job as a freelance facilitator. Even though it meant a fair bit of unpaid time while I learned the ropes as, along with dance sessions, I would also be required to facilitate rhythm sessions, I knew it was the right next step.

So, within two weeks of settling into my new home, I was not only attending a regular yoga class and learning how to drum, I was also teaching dance, supporting the music facilitators and making new friends with people who shared my new outlook on life. Moving to Brighton was definitely a good move.

A couple of times a month, I boosted my income by assisting my friend Leo on his Food Intolerance stand at the Mind Body Soul shows. It also gave me a chance to deepen my knowledge about the different methods of health care I had become interested in. The shows took place at different spots around the country and that is how I ended up one rainy morning in Maidstone – the day Mr Right wandered into my life!

As it happened, it rained so much that day that the show was unusually quiet. After an hour of standing around chatting to Leo and rearranging the stand several times, there were still hardly any punters to talk to, so I went for a wander around the show. There were lots of different stands offering crystals, meditation courses, iridology, reflexology, aura reading, energy-enhancing jewellery, colour therapy. All of these had become familiar and normal in my life over the last few years and it felt good to wander around with a more informed attitude. I was happier now and my health had improved a lot. I had the confidence to sort out the wheat from the chaff, after all my crazy experiences of the pitfalls and wonders of the world of natural health. Like any other areas in life, there are authentic practitioners as well as people with rather fewer scruples, or simply delusions of grandeur.

Desperation no longer blinded me and ruled how I lived my life. I felt really comfortable not being 'a dancer', something that was unthinkable in the past and akin to becoming a nobody. I was enjoying facilitating workshops and working with music and was at ease being a novice and seeing what would unfold in life, rather than trying to work out what was going to happen next all the time.

After a free reflexology taster and sampling a few fresh juices, I got back to Leo's stand. I was standing staring into space whilst Leo chatted to the only punter that had showed any interest in us that morning, when an Indian man wandered around the corner and made a beeline for our stand. He had a side-to-side sway in his steady walk and his hands were clamped casually behind his back as if he was taking his morning constitutional around his village. His deep brown eyes were sparkling in his gentle face, as if he had just been told a humorous secret. He was looking straight at me as if he was about to share it. A funny thought jumped into my head: *I've known him for thousands of years.*

I smiled back as he stopped in front of me. We chatted about the show being quiet and I learned that his name was Jyotish, although most people called him Josh and he had his own stand and was offering Indian head massage. His skin was a warm brown colour and his jet-black hair was shiny and long and tied back in a pony tail. His features were strong and exotic; in fact he looked more Peruvian than Indian. Much later, I learned from him that he was also having a strange feeling that he knew me really well. It was different from any other encounter I had ever had. It was an under-the-earth connection, more like being reconciled with a long-lost friend. After chatting for a while, we reached that awkward point when he needed to go back to his stand and we both wanted to find a way to take things a bit further but didn't want to be too obvious.

As it happened, Leo came to the rescue by asking me if I wanted to take the Indian head massage that Jyotish owed him, in return for a food intolerance test he had done for him at the last show, so we agreed that I should come to his stand toward the end of the day when he had a free slot. I spent the rest of the day clock-watching with a warm feeling in my belly, going over and over the conversation we had had. When the time finally came, I zipped over to his stand.

The massage was beautiful. His strong hands eased away my tension and I fell into a deeply peaceful place. We had a wonderful chat afterwards about life and its strange twists and turns. He was so easy to talk to. His voice was soft and gentle and I felt peaceful just being around him. Once again, we turned into bashful teenagers when it was time for me to get back to the stand and help Leo pack up.

"Erm, I guess I'll see you at the London show in two weeks' time then," he said clumsily.

"Yeah, sure... erm, see you then," I mumbled, turning beetroot red before running off.

The next two weeks passed in a mixture of excitement and apprehension. I kept looking at the Mind Body and Soul programme, at where his stand was going to be, so I could casually walk past and see him again. I wondered whether he was feeling the same. He had seemed interested in me but I could have been imagining it all.

I was put out of my misery when I bumped into him just as I arrived at the London show and, after a brief hello, he asked if I would go to dinner with him on the Saturday evening, which was the second day of the show.

That Saturday evening was the start of our relationship – or, I guess I should say, our courtship. We had a wonderful dinner and he came back to Brighton and we talked way into the night. I learned that he had surfed and been a chef for most of his life, travelling round the world with these two passions, learning about different cultures, which led him to want to study natural medicine. When his father died a few years back, he stopped travelling and went to be with his mother in Birmingham. He had qualified in aromatherapy and

Indian head massage and was currently studying a form of body work called Zero Balancing and another mode of healing known as Eden Energy Medicine. I found him fascinating. He seemed so self-sufficient and easy to be with. He stayed on the sofa that night and we didn't even so much as hug each other goodnight. In fact, our relationship had a very slow start and it was months before our first kiss.

I was used to whirlwind starts to relationships. I tended to fall in love quickly and, unfortunately, out again with the same intensity. This meeting was different. It felt real and deep and sustainable, something to be cherished. It still feels like that to this day.

Not long after we met, Josh took me to meet his teacher, Donna Eden, another introduction that was pivotal in my life. Donna was on her yearly visit to London and was presenting her work at the Mind Body Spirit Festival in London.

We were in the queue outside the conference room when I heard a screech of delight and Josh was suddenly wrapped up in a swoop of velvet.

"Jyotish! Oh, my goodness, oh, how amazing, oh, it's so good to see you!" I saw that this loud American voice belonged to a small, buxom woman, who I guessed was around mid forties (I later learned she was mid fifties), with blonde curls, a youthful grin and pretty, dancing eyes. She had more clothes on than I had ever seen anyone wear, layers and layers of chiffon and velvet.

I hadn't heard anyone call Josh by his real name at this point and it reminded me that I didn't really know him that well. I stood and watched this exuberant woman gushing over this guy who, so far, had seemed pretty sane and wondered what I was letting myself in for. It wasn't the picture I had formed in my head when Josh told me his revered teacher of Eden Energy Medicine was coming to England. Donna eventually let go of Josh and, when she was introduced to me, she swooped me up in a warm embrace with tears in her eyes.

"Oh Lianne, it's so good to meet you. Oh, oh, oh, how lovely!" She spun around and faced Josh again, appearing to forget why she was in this queue and then just as quickly whooshed away, waving and smiling to us. I grinned wildly and waved back, feeling completely bewildered.

We found our places near the front of the conference room and after her introduction, which was like watching an excited child about to go to Disneyland, the workshop began and Donna started to bring volunteers onto the stage. Within a few minutes, I was utterly enchanted by this passionate woman with an enormous capacity for love and an incredible gift. It became apparent very quickly that Donna could see people's energy as clearly as she could see their physical bodies. The accuracy of her observations and the humble way she offered help with pain and tension, as well as serious illnesses, left me awestruck. Her demonstrations were peppered with inspiring stories and the packed audience learned numerous tips and techniques to balance and heal their own bodies and keep themselves in good shape.

Watching Donna Eden work was my first understanding of how the anatomy of energy is as complex and intricate as our physical bodies. She demonstrated beautifully how, with a little knowledge, this powerful, innate healing force within us is easily accessible.

It was inspiring to know that Donna's early life had been plagued with illness; asthma, ME, MS, a heart attack in her early thirties, to the point where she spent two years in a wheelchair and was told to put her affairs in order by the doctors, who said no more could be done.

It was only then that she started to experiment with her gift to be able to see the flow of her energy and how she could manipulate and enhance it using her hands and thoughts. She found ways to help her body to heal by itself and defied her doctors' predictions. In fact, she proved the absolute contrary and has spent decades growing younger, stronger and healthier and teaching thousands of others how to do the same.

Donna is living proof of how much joy and fulfilment is available for us to tap into. To this day, I have never met a more vibrant, joyful person. She is now in her seventies, and still travels the world, ignited by her passion to inspire people to harness their own energy to experience good health and vitality.

A few weeks after meeting Josh, I finally finished *The Artist's Way* course that had taken longer than the twelve allotted weeks, due to my big move. I read over the pages I had written after the dull, grey period in which I had my revelation that it was my attitude to life that needed to change. In my free-flow writing the following morning, I had blurted out everything I was going to create from that day on. I stated that I wanted a man who had the same interests and view on life as me and was willing to work on problems that came up in our relationship, instead of blaming or walking away. Someone who didn't need to be rescued and didn't want to rescue me. I also said I wanted to live in a beautiful flat that was above the ground floor, with lovely views and which felt like a safe haven to come back to at the end of the day. A home in a location where I could expand my horizons and discover parts of myself that I hadn't considered yet. A place where I could make money easily and enjoy a great social life.

I had remembered the feeling of clarity and determination I had as I wrote, but not the actual detail. As I read it back less than two months later, I was stunned at how much of it had manifested already. It was a great wink from the universe that somehow I had got myself on track.

Chapter Eighteen

BRANCHING OUT

Josh eventually moved into the flat with me and the next seven or so years were all about expanding our work, enjoying all that Brighton had to offer and getting to know each other. As many people experience, once the honeymoon period was over it was time to bring out the worst in each other! Relationships take commitment and a willingness to give each other space to grow and there have been many times when we have found ourselves staring at each other, defeated and exhausted and wondering why on earth we were bothering. I think that the under-the-earth connection we both felt kept us together. We both knew that the battle we were playing out was inside ourselves; that we would find this conflict elsewhere if it wasn't with each other. Our commitment forced each other to look at the sides of our nature we would rather ignore. I am grateful for the time and effort we put in and, after seventeen years together, Our relationship feels solid and honest.

It was my daily practice that kept me stable when things got turbulent, giving me time to reflect. In the past, I would have moved on and blamed him, or gone on a party binge, or found a job conveniently in another country. However, as I felt happier and more secure, I found I was more willing to look at myself. It only takes one person to change a pattern in a relationship and, knowing we were both committed to freeing ourselves up regardless of the other, it helped when one of us got stuck in the blame game.

It was amazing to experience time and time again that when I focused on changing my reaction to something, or found a way to fulfil a need in myself, rather than trying to control or expect him to fulfil something for me, the conflict dissolved. We seemed almost to take it in turns that one of us would wake up and stop playing tit for tat and therefore carry us through.

Over the years, life began to feel easier and more fluid, my health improved, my financial situation improved, my relationship with Josh got stronger and I felt more and more at ease with who I was.

Work morphed into various stages over the years, until I was doing an eclectic mix of all the things I was interested in and that had helped me.

I qualified as a yoga instructor and that led to both Josh and I having regular work at a retreat centre. As well as teaching yoga and meditation, we also created workshops on self-development. This kind of work spread into the corporate world, where we led classes on stress management and health. I continued to work with Red Zebra for a while. Although I had thoroughly enjoyed it, they were growing and getting busier and I didn't want to embrace it as a career. I took heed from mistakes I had made in the past and followed my gut. Although it was hard to leave, as I really enjoyed the job, I wanted to some space to see what else life had to offer. It wasn't long after that I got the chance to choreograph and play in a samba band. Since then, I have trusted that feeling to close something a number of times and have always been pleasantly surprised at how many doors open when you willingly close another. I see it as trust in one message; allowing me to hear the next one.

A twist of fate also brought me a regular choreography job, which gave me the creative outlet I needed and my link to the world of dance. After my sabbatical, I was ready to experience this world with my passion renewed and my desperation diminished.

After sending out my CV to a whole load of companies, one was picked up in Essex by Martin Berger. Martin was working as head of entertainment for four family holiday parks and his ambition was to improve the standard of the productions, which at that time were pretty dire. When my CV landed on his desk the morning he had decided to search for a choreographer, he called me and I went down to Dorset to meet him and he offered me the job.

It turned out to be a great opportunity and perfectly suited the lifestyle I was creating in Brighton. I was contracted twice a year to choreograph winter and summer seasons. I loved working with Martin, who was a musician, singer and writer. He was talented, funny and good company and we seemed to bounce off each other really well. We created over forty shows in the nine years we worked together. It gave me a huge creative outlet and a chance to research many different styles of dance and, as the reputation of the company grew, we got to work with some incredibly gifted singers and dancers.

Chapter Nineteen

GROWING UP

As my relationship with Josh strengthened and life became more stable, the subject of children became more obvious. I always felt I would have children at some point and had decided long ago that I would wait until I was older so I could enjoy my dancing career. However, my plans for 'doing it later' were also shaped by the fact that I had always seen having a family as the end of freedom. Although I had questioned almost everything else I had been told about life, I remained steadfast in my belief that once children came along, that was it. I would be housebound, become boring and feel trapped. However the desire to be a mum was growing and I was thirty-eight and couldn't put it off much longer.

Josh, who is someone who isn't at all bound by time and space, was feeling no sense of urgency and was happy to start trying when we were ready (in other words, he was leaving the monstrous decision to me!). So we carried on using a contraceptive and I kept hoping somehow it would just happen so I wouldn't have to think about it.

Of course, it didn't happen like that. As the subject of partaking in bringing the next generation into the world loomed silently in my awareness, broader questions about life and why we live like we do also cropped up more frequently. I began to notice many people I was coming across in my work, at retreats, in the corporate world and in day to day life, who were settling for second best; relationships that didn't quite work but were okay, jobs that went from being plain pointless, to stupidly demanding. People doing stuff that they never really wanted to do but were too institutionalised to move on. These kinds of observations had always been with me, but they got stronger with my desire to be a mum. If I had kids, I wanted to raise my children in a different way, a way in which they could be free from the constraints of institutions and the 'have tos' and 'shoulds' that nobody really wants to go along with and yet somehow just does. I began to research other cultures and different ways of child-rearing in order to understand more about human nature. It was through this research that I came across a book called *The Continuumn Concept*, by Jean Liedloff.

In the book, she describes her observations of a Native American culture that had never had contact with the western world. Their community were good-natured, peaceful and happy. They enjoyed life to the full and every aspect of village life was like a celebration. She noticed that as soon as babies were born they went in a sling and that life, for the mother, resumed as normal. The babies went to work with mama, slept with mama, were attended to whenever they cried and were left to crawl away when they were ready, knowing they could come back to mama whenever they needed her. In short, all their needs were met.

She noted that all the children grew up confident that they had a place in their community. Contrary to the belief in our culture, interdependence until the child was ready to find his or her own feet created independent, confident individuals that contributed happily to the community and village life. Children were never coerced, manipulated or scolded, they were treated with the same respect and kindness that was given to adults. Adults also had their needs met; even when they had very young children, they continued to enjoy village life, have plenty of adult company and the support of the community as they tended to their children and contributed to their community.

There was no conflict between children or adults and, although no-one was forced to do anything, everyone naturally participated in village life. Children became willing members of the workforce, as play naturally expanded into joining the adults in their light approach to even the most strenuous of tasks. They equated responsibility and contribution, with enjoyment and a sense of belonging. I was fascinated by the book, as it suggested that so much of what we take for granted as human nature is simply a product of our culture and the way we raise our children. It released me from my restricted views of what it meant to become a parent.

It was on my thirty-ninth birthday that we decided to start trying for a baby. Ever since I was old enough to think about having babies, I'd had age forty in mind as the right time for me. It never occurred to me that I was leaving it too late. I always thought I would conceive quickly and fully expected to be pregnant the first month we tried. Little did I know what a big journey lay ahead.

When we thought of a family, both of us imagined a place with a garden closer to countryside, where our kids could run wild, explore woods, splash in rivers and climb trees. It was also difficult to leave fun-filled Brighton, so we decided that the baby would move us. Eventually, we would fall pregnant and the incentive to provide our dream environment for our family would move us on. The first few months when I didn't conceive, I was surprised but still optimistic. After six months, though, I started to question myself and ask what was holding me back? I figured it was all to do with timing. It wouldn't be long, it couldn't be. I was fast approaching forty, the age I had decided I would have a child and there was no doubt in my mind that I would be a mum one day.

Unfortunately, as much as we dreamed and hoped month after month, year after year, we still had no real reason to leave a flat that was perfect for a childless couple. And as time went on, it became more of an issue for me. When we were away on jobs, I would sit at dinner tables hoping no-one would ask me if I had children, or that the conversation wouldn't turn to other people's children. Of course it always did. Everybody had kids, even people who didn't want kids had kids. It was easy to get pregnant. My mum had done it three times and my sisters did it easily enough and had five kids between them to prove it. Everywhere I looked, there seem to be a newborn. Everybody was doing it! Why couldn't I?

I still couldn't quite believe I wasn't conceiving, especially as I knew with every bone in my body that

I was going to be a mum. However, I still took the 'believe in God and tie up your camel' approach and, alongside cultivating inner peace and acceptance, we turned to alternative medicine to help me conceive. Through recommendation, we found two very gifted practitioners, a cranial sacral osteopath and a reflexologist.

Both Josh and I saw these practitioners independently of each other and we were always comforted by the accuracy of their observations on how we were feeling and what was going on in our lives, simply by tuning in to our energy. This approach of gently preparing the body and releasing anything that may be preventing me from conceiving, resonated with me. I didn't want invasive medical procedures, so going to the GP for help was out of the question.

We also secured the rope around our camel by arranging our flat to be more inviting to a child. We made a set of shelves available to put nappies and baby clothes on. Josh bought a teddy bear, a maternity dress and presented me with flowers for Mother's Day. We planned how we would adapt our work and lives once the kids came along, and kept visualising ourselves having a family. We even had sex!

Guiding life in this way had become a normal part of our lives. It was the way we shaped our work, planned holidays or drew certain events to us, so we were pretty confident that the baby would soon be with us.

As time went on, though and my fortieth, forty-first and forty-second birthday passed, my confidence in my instinct that this would happen at the right time was getting chipped away by the inevitable fact that I had a body clock, and most women who were going to conceive already had done so, way before they were at the age I was.

My anxiety was mounting, although Josh remained steady in his belief that it would happen, which sometimes I found comforting and at others infuriating. We made a few attempts to find home outside Brighton, thinking that would tempt our little one to put in an appearance. The idea of being closer to our families often gave us some incentive. Mine were still living up north in Manchester and Josh's were mostly in Birmingham and had been since they had moved there from Uganda in the Sixties. We had a few trips and explored Shropshire, Cheshire and Hebden Bridge in Yorkshire, but we always ended up back in Brighton. Without a doubt, it was difficult to move on. There is something different about Brighton. Being popular with musicians, artists and natural health practitioners, as well as trendy business people, students and families, makes it lively, vibrant, alternative and quirky. Plus, we had a great flat at a reasonably priced rent, thirty seconds from the beach and two minutes from the centre of the city. (Excuse my inner estate agent; she pops out from time to time!)

So we stayed where we were and trusted that one day something would happen that would give us good reason to move. If it wasn't a baby, we were also open to an irresistible career break beckoning us to fulfil our destiny in a foreign land, or an angel landing on our bed in the middle of the night, whispering the instruction, "Go pack your bags and head west".

Then lo and behold, our sign to move on eventually came to us. A sign that was the result of an experience in South Africa...

Chapter Twenty

SAFARI SO GOODIE

I was booked to fly to Cape Town at the end of the summer I turned forty-three. I had made it my visualisation throughout the summer that I would have to call the company and announce that I could no longer do the job because I was in the early stages of pregnancy and didn't want to risk a long haul flight.

I spent the whole summer with that thought in my head and regularly imagined picking up the phone to say, "I've got good news and bad news. The bad news is, I am not going to be able to go to South Africa. The good news is, we are going to have the baby we have been longing for!"

The job involved flying to Cape Town for four days, to create a piece of theatre in a beautiful outdoor arena and then, those wishing to stay on could fly to Johannesburg, where a light aircraft would take us to to Phinda Private Game Reserve for a four-day Safari. It was a dream job and a longstanding ambition of mine to go on Safari and this was a real opportunity to do it in a style that would normally be way out of my holiday budget. Knowing that I would rather give all that up to be pregnant, was proof that it was number one on my list and I was hoping it would also be proof enough to the little soul I still felt sure would eventually be inside me.

However, two weeks before I was due to fly to South Africa, my body informed me that there was no need to make that call. I knew I wasn't doing myself any favours by being so calculating and making these deadlines. Josh never wavered in his optimism. He kept reassuring me that he had no doubt that we would be parents and we just had to trust that it would happen at the right time. I knew that no matter what, it was important to carry on believing, it was the only chance we had. It's a massive test of faith, however, when your heart and soul say one thing and your body keeps telling you another.

As expected, the job was an experience of a lifetime. After four fun days of work in Cape Town, four of us went on Safari. My companions were all women who I knew well, having worked on various jobs with them in recent years. There was Shelley, a tiny, energetic, frighteningly efficient and very naughty young woman; Peta, who can only be labelled as 'one hell of a broad', 'witty' being an understatement as she was able to slip seamlessly between bawdy Australian gal to sexy sophisticated lady at the drop of a hat; and Esperide, a beautiful, feisty and fiery Italian woman with an unrivalled passion for life. Needless to say, I had a wonderful time with this eclectic bunch of women, lots of laughs, a few tears and great company.

We headed off in high spirits after the success of the job, full of the excitement of what would be a brand new experience for all of us.

The four days that followed are stamped in my soul as one of the most memorable times of my life and I still enjoy reminiscing and immersing myself in every detail.

Sitting in an open top jeep in the African bush only metres away from wild and exquisitely beautiful animals; the smell of fresh earth in the air and feeling the early morning sun starting to burn through, hinting at the baking temperatures forecast for the afternoon; and then being in the pitch black after sundown, sipping a gin and tonic and feeling the welcome coolness of the night air as it coaxed the nocturnal creatures to perform a concert of the most enchanting music. Sounds of the wild. Nature at its most awesome.

It was a heavenly experience. I sat mesmerised and moved to tears every morning, as we headed out as the dawn was breaking, only returning when the day got too hot to handle. In the very early evening, we would watch the sun go down, then roam around the bush in the pitch darkness. We travelled through stunning landscapes to see elephants, the sheer size of them taking my breath away no matter how many times I saw them. There were rhinos, comfortable and proud of their hefty bulk. Hippos, the comedians of the animal world, hiding under the water with only their eyes visible, waiting for the moment you look away before they rise effortlessly out of the water, release a great gaping yawn and sink back down again quickly, with a smug grin, as you manage to spin around in time to snap yet another picture of the surface of the lake. We saw giraffes, every graceful movement like a perfectly choreographed ballet, walking with every inch of their bodies connected, a divine ripple of movement integrating them from their finely-boned faces to their tiny, dainty feet. A cheetah with her three cubs tumbling and playing in the long grass whilst she kept diligent watch, ready to spring into action and protect her precious family at any given moment. We even saw a baboon, which was rare for the area we were in.

It was humbling to witness the natural order intact, life left to follow its natural rhythms, night and day, rest and play, movement and stillness. Also, the easy acceptance of life and death and the healthy response of fight or flight; reacting to the alert of danger and, once it has passed, returning to the natural state of peaceful presence, happy in the moment. It is a rhythm our modern-day world is often so far removed from, with our twenty-four-hour days packed with busyness, environments cut off from nature, segregated into our boxes of homes, offices, schools and nurseries, and artificial lights day and night. How much of the true beauty and purpose of life do we miss out on, being so cut off from the circadian rhythms that are designed to nurture and connect us so that we thrive, rather than just survive, this precious life?

My favourite of favourites were the lions and we were lucky enough to come across the big daddy on more than one occasion. One time, he was with his two lionesses; with him leading, they slunk arrogantly past our jeep, almost close enough to touch on their way to drink from the river. Another morning, we found him sitting beside a lake with his two equally exotic sons. An eerie silence fell amongst us as we sat and took in the scene that was almost biblical. Majestic and defiant as they all were, there was no doubting who was the daddy; he sat slightly away from his sons, his great mane framing his powerful face. He was the only one who would mate with the other females whilst he ruled. The females would hunt for him and, as the king of the jungle, he had no predators, leaving him to sleep for up to sixteen hours a day and lie around looking gorgeous. I looked to my left and saw Shelley wiping tears away. I put my arm around her and we just sat in silence, no words needed, just sharing the depths of the moment.

"I can't live any longer without an animal in my life," I stated dramatically to Josh on my return. "We have to get a dog."

"Okay, let's do it then," he replied

"What?" I had made the statement dramatically because I was fully expecting to come up against resistance. "But you don't like dogs!" I challenged.

"It's not that I don't like dogs, it's just I'm not into them like you are," he said defensively. "I can take them or leave them."

When I was a child, it was my dream to have a dog and, after years of pleading and leaving cute puppy pictures around the house, I came down one Christmas morning to find a little black cocker spaniel that we named Scamp. He became the centre of my world as I was growing up. As I flew back from South Africa, the magic memories of every animal that I had encountered in wild and mysterious Africa brought me to remembering how special my relationship with Scamp was. The games we played, all the secrets I told him, all the special moments that had enhanced my childhood. The prospect of having that in my life again was very exciting.

We went for a walk on the beach and spent the afternoon talking about the pros and cons of having a dog. We worked away from home a fair bit, so that would mean finding suitable dog minders. We had been free to do as we liked for the last ten years and this would be a big commitment. As we walked and talked through all the plusses and minuses, we came to the conclusion that we were actually both fed up with getting up in the morning and only having to think about ourselves. We wanted to have the experience of having to think about another being, so having a dependent would be good for us.

By the time we got home, we were excited and ready to make a commitment to a new adventure. I checked our diaries. I had only two overseas jobs booked in up until the end of January, so there was a perfect window of time to get a dog settled in. I had the feeling that the universe was with us on this one.

Chapter Twenty-One

FINDING LEELA

Once we had committed to getting a dog, deciding on the breed was a no-brainer. My sisters had three working cocker spaniels between them and since the dogs joined the family, most of my visits home were centred around dog walking, dog talking, dog stroking and general dogginess. In fact, Maxine's husband Rick, swears we all suffer from dog Tourette's syndrome, as we are unable to get through an hour without saying something doggy-related. As we gush over the latest members of the family, he has a habit of yelling random phrases from behind his paper, like "Poo bags!" or "Waggy tail!"

As my sisters' dogs are male, we decided to go with the same sex, simply because that was what we were used to. The other specification to narrow down the search was for an un-docked tail. As ever, our preference was to leave things as nature intended, especially as the tail plays a big part in the way dogs communicate and express their personalities.

Since we didn't have a garden, a rescue dog was out of the question so, once the preliminaries were decided upon, I spent many a joyful evening scouring the internet, looking at gorgeous puppies.

I was waiting for the 'that's the one' feeling I was sure I would feel, when I laid eyes on the puppy we were destined to share our lives with. One evening, I was just about to close the computer down, feeling a bit weary, having spent two hours puppy-hunting with no twinges being offered from my intuition, when I spotted an advert and felt I should just check one more before I gave up for the night.

I clicked on the screen and a photo of four adorable little bitch puppies took my breath away. They were black with white markings on their noses, chests and paws and looked almost identical, four little barrels of fun. There was one on the end with her tongue curled up to lick her nose and she was looking straight into the camera. When my eyes fell on her, my stomach and heart did a little dance. This was the feeling I'd been waiting for and it was totally unexpected, as I had been on the lookout for a male. However, I followed the feeling and called the breeders, who were based in Worcester.

A woman answered the phone and informed me that the puppies were now eight weeks old, two of them had been viewed and bought already and there were people coming to see the other two at the weekend. At that point, I couldn't bring myself to ask her if the one at the end with her tongue sticking out was still for sale, as I was too afraid of the answer. Buying a puppy over the phone was not an option (which is the sign of a good breeder), and we had the problem of having to leave for France the next day to work for ten days and then go immediately to Kent to work at a retreat weekend.

All in all, it meant not being able to get to Worcester for another two weeks! I resigned myself to the fact that I had to trust and hand things over to fate.

Easier said than done! Did I really believe that the one at the end was ours and would be waiting for us in two weeks' time? Or did I think it was a load of bunkum and the best thing to do would be to feign illness, cancel everything and bomb up there and get her NOW! Well, I can honestly say that the answer to both was yes! Which was rather confusing, to say the least. Josh was in for a less than peaceful couple of weeks.

I got back from France after our ten-day stint and called Worcester straight away. The breeder informed me that there was one left! We still had the retreat weekend to do so we couldn't get there until Tuesday, but at least there was one left. Then she added, "There are some people coming from Liverpool on Saturday to see her."

I felt sick. "Which one is left?" I asked in a tight voice.

"The one at the end with her tongue sticking out," she replied.

My heart and stomach glided together once more but this time pirouetted into my throat. I had that split feeling again, as one half of me scrambled through desperate plans to jump in the car now, seize the puppy and travel back overnight, or cancel the retreat, or get my sister to drive down and get her or, or... Whilst that was going on, the other half of me went very calm and, having heard it confirmed that the puppy I knew was mine from the moment I saw her was indeed the only one left, I felt absolutely confident that this was meant to be.

Over the babble of thoughts, I heard myself arranging that if the puppy was still there on Sunday, she would leave a message on our home phone number as my mobile reception was unpredictable at the retreat, and we would get back to her. I put the phone down and spent the rest of the evening listening to the voice of calm and wisdom vs. the voice of doom and gloom battle it out in my head.

"It's fine, just trust, it's a big step and at this point, if it's right, she will be there for us on Tuesday."

"Who in their right mind would drive from Liverpool to Worcester, see a beautiful little puppy and say, 'No thanks, we wanted one a bit cuter than that' and then drive all the way back again empty-handed?"

"Somehow, they won't take her. Everything else points to her being ours, the gut feeling, the fact that she is the only one still left, us having a lull of two and a half months of minimum travel in order to settle her in. The universe is with us on this one."

"There is no God."

"There is, and he likes me."

"There isn't, and if there was, he would be out there saving the world from disaster, not providing you with a puppy."

"No, he wouldn't, God doesn't... Oh, for goodness' sake, go away!"

"Fine, be disappointed on Tuesday then."

"I won't be! Think positive, you get what you think about."

"Where's that million quid then?"

"On its way."

"How come you don't look like Jennifer Anniston yet?"

"Oh, shut up and go to sleep!"

That weekend, we were working at Oxon Hoath, a beautiful retreat centre in Kent and one of my favourite places on the planet. Josh and I had been developing our work for ten weekends a year for the past eight years in this old stately home. Set in eighty acres of gardens and countryside, it was both grand and simple. Our fondness for the old place is shared by the other therapists and teachers that form the staff for the weekend retreats, as well as the housekeepers and guests.

I usually enjoy every minute of these weekends. The place is timeless and peaceful and the pace slow, a perfect environment to teach practices based on cultivating these qualities. Although there is a sense of anticipation on the Friday evening, by Saturday lunchtime it feels that we have all been there winding down and de-stressing for months. This particular weekend was a challenge because, instead of sinking into the timeless zone, I wanted to speed everything up and get to Sunday evening as quickly as possible.

As usual, I started off on Saturday morning teaching my yoga class in the beautiful dance studio, its huge sash windows framing the stunning views of the rose garden and fields beyond. I was twitchy and found myself clock-watching, something I hadn't done for a long time.

"Stay present and enjoy the posture," I heard myself saying, as I noticed it was only 10.20, still another forty minutes to go. I grappled with my wandering mind and tried not to plan to run to the toilet at the end of my yoga class, so I could phone home and check the answer machine.

"Be in this perfect moment, no need to rush into the next, be happy where you are," I said, talking to myself more than anybody else and feeling annoyed at my inability to follow my own simple instruction.

I managed to get myself reasonably settled by the end of the class and was pleased to be able to keep myself in check through the meditation session. The deep breathing and observation helped me to let go of the anxiety and by the time I taught the movement class, I was feeling light and easy. That still didn't stop me reaching for my mobile the moment the class had finished and the guests had left the room. There were no messages at home.

"Nice morning?" Josh inquired at lunchtime

"Yeah, how about you?"

"Yeah, good, met some interesting people." Josh had been doing one-on-one treatments of Zero Balancing and Energy Medicine.

"No news from Worcester yet," I said, trying to sound okay about it, as I knew I would annoy Josh if I got obsessive.

"Just leave it until tonight now. There's no point in

phoning every five minutes, you'll only get stressed out for no reason." He knew I was obsessing. I smiled weakly and agreed.

After lunch, Josh went back to his treatment room and I went for a walk in the grounds. I practised a walking meditation, but kept finding myself wondering if the people from Liverpool had set off to buy our puppy. Each time, I rewrote the story and had them decide not to go because they had found another breeder closer to where they lived. I managed not to phone home again.

In the afternoon, Josh and I taught Energy Medicine together. I enjoyed teaching what I most needed myself, simple techniques to de-stress the body and clear the mind. I had my final session in the evening – Nature's Rhythms, a free-flow dance class and I indulged myself in music that swept me away for a couple of hours, letting go of any worries that our little puppy was now on her way to Liverpool.

During the last ten minutes, when we lay on the floor breathing deeply and enjoying the after-glow of having danced our socks off, a little snuffly puppy face kept appearing under my eyelids and my doubts returned. I phoned home one more time before I went to bed and found there were three messages! I tried to calm my thumping heart as I listened through them. Two were from Mum, who had forgotten we were away and the third was a wrong number, somebody called Bob trying to contact Gina. I went to bed and lay awake feeling sad and annoyed with Bob and Gina and wishing I'd opted to be unprofessional and gone up to Worcester this weekend.

Sunday passed equally slowly, although I did manage to keep my mind from wandering. I stayed focused on what I was doing and felt grateful for all the hours I had put in practising this skill. These were the kinds of times when it paid off. I may not have been terribly happy but at least I wasn't driving myself insane.

In the evening, we had our staff Christmas party. About twenty therapists, workshop facilitators and house staff gathered in the library after the guests had gone home. There was a roaring fire and plenty of food and drink. It was a lively event but the festive spirit wasn't with me. Teri, the house manager, a fast-talking, quick-witted woman from New Jersey, was doing some fantastic impressions of the therapists to raucous laughter when I popped out of the library and sat on the main staircase to phone home one last time. It was now 9.30pm and I decided that if there wasn't a message by now, it meant that I had been over-optimistic and it was time to face it. I dialled our number and tapped in the pin to access the answer machine. There was a message. I swallowed in anticipation as I recognised the breeder's voice.

"Just to let you know the people didn't turn up over the weekend so we still have the one puppy left."

As I pressed the repeat button and listened to the message again, I felt sick. Had I heard that right? Or had wishful thinking caused me to have an aural hallucination? I heard the same message again and felt a warm glow spread through my body. She was ours! My gut feeling had been right. How could I have ever doubted it?

I ran back and told Josh and his face lit up. "Merry Christmas," he said, smothering me with a big bear hug. He knew how much this meant to me. Little did he know then how much it would end up meaning to him, too. We spent the rest of the evening embracing the festive season at full throttle!

Chapter Twenty-Two

MAN PLANS...

The next day felt like it was going backwards; a whole day before we could get in the car and go to Worcester. We drove back to Brighton feeling worse for wear but still in good spirits and in the afternoon, we went to the pet shop. It was exciting buying all her things, a bed, toys, food, bowls, collar and lead.

"Shall we get her one of these as well?' Josh stood dangling a fluffy black and white dice above the over-flowing basket he was carrying.

"Don't you think we have enough now?" I replied, thinking about the size of the flat and wondering where all this gear was going to fit.

"We want her to feel welcome," he said, eyes shining with excitement. I was beginning to realise that this was no 'take them or leave them' kind of guy speaking. I took the dice off him and dropped it in the basket. I wondered what it was like finding out you were pregnant and then having to wait a whole nine months to get to see your baby. I could hardly wait another minute and, having bought all the stuff, it felt like torture not to be able to use it for at least another sixteen hours!

We spent the evening deciding where everything should go. We were going to crate-train her for a few months, so she could have her own little 'cave' to go to whenever she needed and we would have a safe place to put her when we needed to go out. The breeder kept her in a crate in the house and said she had no trouble putting her down to sleep and had often left her on her own in the daytime whilst she went out. Dogs don't tend to soil their own crates, either, so it would be a good way to toilet-train her.

We placed toilet-training pads in the bathroom and the plan was to take her to the pad when she woke up and do the same after she had been playing for a while, which is when they tend to go. If she did it anywhere else, we would scold the poo for being in the wrong place, put it on the training pad where we wanted it, and praise it (yes, praise it!) and reward her with a treat. The psychology behind this is that the puppy will want to put the poo where it pleases you and therefore be rewarded itself. Wees would be soaked up with the pad (whilst scolding it of course,) and then the pad would be placed in the bathroom, accompanied by lots of praise and a treat for the puppy.

Our plan was to start with the training pad in the toilet and then, once she used it regularly, we would slowly edge it down the hall to outside the front door, where she would get used to going and sitting by the front door when she wanted to use it. Easy-peasy! My sisters had trained their dogs reasonably quickly like this, so we knew the system worked. The only difference was that they had gardens and had trained their dogs without the pads. Seeing as we were on the first floor, we needed to allow her time to strengthen her bladder and gain bowel control. My sister Kaye had said that initially, we should put the toilet pad down wherever she chose to poo, but we decided that we could choose for her. The toilet was the easiest and the most obvious place.

Our flat was in good order; we prided ourselves on the space we had created. We used the Feng Shui map as a guide on where to place things. Although we didn't follow it to a tee, it was fun to explore its impact. Basically, any space is sectioned into eight, with a ninth space in the centre. Each section symbolises areas of life; relationships, creativity, career, helpful friends, wealth, contemplation, our ancestors and inspiration. For us, Feng Shui had become a way to guide our lives and serve as a reminder that we have a hand in our destiny, and life's not just a series of random events.

At that time, in our wealth corner we had a water fountain to symbolise easy flow, a golden egg for fertility and a laughing Buddha called Dave after my dad, to represent fun and love. That evening, we added a fluffy dice to symbolise good luck for our new arrival. We also placed a rose quartz in the relationship area, to help the bonding process.

"What are we going to call her then?" Josh said, as we settled on to the settee for the evening.

I hesitated. I knew her name. It had boomed out in my head the moment I laid eyes on her photo. It was the name we had planned to call our daughter if we had one. I don't know why it felt right to give it away. It wasn't because I had given up hope, it just felt like a kind of surrender. I paused a moment and then said cautiously, "I think we should give her the name Leela."

Josh looked at me for a long moment while I desperately tried to read his face, I didn't want to hurt him or have him misinterpret the reason behind it. I started to explain, "It's not that I have given up hope," when he cut across me.

"That feels right," he said quietly, "she looks like a Leela." He put his arm around me and we sat in silence for a long time, just watching the candle burn down.

Leela, the Sanskrit word I had first heard from my Brazilian percussion teacher. , My favourite translation of it is 'Divine dance of life': to me, that means going with the flow and living life magically.

So now we were about to hand over that heavenly name to our ten-week-old spaniel – not quite what we had imagined in our ideal baby-naming ceremony, but hey, sometimes you have to let life live you.

Chapter Twenty-Three

GOD LAUGHS!

The next morning, we were up early and on our way. The journey went reasonably quickly considering the amount of energy needed to contain my excitement. As we pulled into the breeders' drive, my heart started to race. I still couldn't quite believe I was finally going to have a dog of my own.

The breeders came out to meet us and introduced themselves as Julie and John. They were warm and friendly and invited us around the back of the house. As they opened the kitchen door, a little brown rowan puppy with blue eyes sprang out and behind her, another pup half the size stumbled over the doorframe and flopped headfirst into the garden. This was Leela. She was even smaller than I thought she would be. Her little, fat puppy body wiggled happily past me, determined to keep up with her companion. Then she suddenly did a U-turn and looked up at me, I bent down to pick her up and fell in love. She was adorable.

After a quick sniff at me, she struggled impatiently to get down and go about her business of exploring the garden. I stopped myself calling her by her name in front of the breeders, as somehow it felt silly that we had already named her. After a few moments, she ran back over to me and I picked her up again. This time, she went still and looked directly into my eyes. She felt so tiny in my hands and I was overwhelmed with how much I loved her already. A few seconds later, she was wiggling to get down again, eager to stay busy having fun.

We went to the kennels where all the other dogs lived and we were pleased to see they were all happy, healthy working dogs and excited to see us. We met Dad, a creamy white, brown-eyed, handsome two-year-old with a ring in his mouth that he apparently carried from morning until night. He looked cheeky and friendly. Then we met Mum, who was stunning, jet black with a longish wavy coat and soulful eyes. There was something about her nature that really touched me. She seemed gentle and wise. She looked at us as if she was checking out who was taking her daughter.

"Don't worry, we'll take good care of your baby," I heard Josh say to her quietly. He was obviously thinking the same as me! It made me smile. Josh has an ingrained respect for mothers and had a special relationship with his own mother until she died, only a few years ago. Now the 'take it or leave it' dog man was talking to this mother with the utmost respect. I had a feeling he was going to be far more involved in Leela's life than he had originally thought.

I knew that it was natural at this point for the pups to move away from their mothers and become independent, but it still felt incredibly sad to be taking her away. We took pictures of Mum and Dad and, promising them both to give her a happy life, we went indoors to have a cup of tea and do the paperwork whilst Leela ran around the garden after the brown rowan.

The moment came to leave and I picked Leela up so Julie and John could say goodbye to her. I snuggled her into my chest. I didn't want her to feel frightened as she left the only home she had ever known in her short ten-week life. She seemed relaxed as we got in the car and it was only when we started to reverse that she started slightly and stared out of the window at Julie and John, as if she realised she was leaving them. I spoke softly to reassure her. She looked at me and started to wag her tail, wiggling like crazy to reach and lick my face. It felt lovely. It was as if she had just realised that I was mum now and had decided to check me out fully.

It took her about fifteen minutes to calm down and she eventually fell asleep on my knee. I stroked and studied her as she slept. I remember thinking, *I want to know every inch of you, every little nook and cranny of your little body and face.* I wanted every part of her to be familiar to me so that if I closed my eyes, I could picture every detail. She lay flat on her back and totally at peace, fitting perfectly along my thighs. *I'll remember this,* I promised myself. *I'll remember how tiny she is now and watch her grow day by day and talk about how she used to fit perfectly on my knee.*

I stroked her soft, chubby belly and wanted to know what she liked, what soothed her when she was nervous, what put her to sleep and what enticed her into play. I had so much to learn about this little creature and I wanted to do right by her, give her a long, happy and healthy life. "Leela." I kept trying out her name and it felt good.

Josh was beaming from ear to ear and kept glancing over.

"What is she doing now?" he would ask every now and again. "Still asleep? Peaceful, isn't she?"

We knew that it could often be traumatic for a pup on their first trip to their new home and were prepared for her to be sick or show signs of distress. There was no need, though; this little Buddha slept peacefully in my arms for the whole three and a half hour journey back. Not a care in the world.

We stopped off at a quiet park when we got back to Brighton, so she could go to the toilet before we got to the flat. We had bought her a red lead and collar and she looked adorable as she bounced over the grass, taking in her new surroundings. We only stayed a few minutes whilst she did the business and then got back in the car, eager to introduce her to her new home.

It was a moment in history when we walked through the doorway of our flat with our little bundle. We put her down in the hallway and she tootled off into the living room, went straight to the wealth corner and did a huge poo! Well, that was that decision settled, then. Contrary to ancient Chinese wisdom, Leela felt that the wealth corner was the perfect place to have a toilet! Fantastic! Whilst she relieved herself, she could look out of the windows, check out what was going on in the street, enjoy the sea views and, according to the Feng Shui belief system, bring more and more of whatever she deposited there into our lives!

With Plan A out of the window, we took the training pad and placed it in our precious wealth corner which was now officially the dog toilet. We decided not to scold the poo on this occasion, as we didn't want it to spoil her first experience of being at home and we felt silly enough as it was, without having to shout "naughty poo!" at the offensive item that happened to be positioned next to Dave the Buddha!

That night, we celebrated with a curry, lit candles and opened a bottle of wine. Leela explored the flat and then fell asleep on my knee again. It had been a big day for all of us. We were now a family of three. We put Leela in her crate that night. Inside it was her new soft bed and the fluffy dice. She went to sleep quite happily and slept until the morning. I, on the other hand, lay awake most of the night and enjoyed going over the day in minute detail. It was hard to resist the temptation to get her out of her crate and cuddle her in bed, but I managed it.

The next morning, we woke early and experienced what became the morning ritual. Leela was obviously awake before us and at the first whiff that we had woken up, she made a little whimper of protest. It was a high-pitched sound and sounded like an indignant, "Why?"

Josh and I looked at each other and smiled and then waited to see what she would do next. One of us moved slightly and she made two whimpers in a high pitch, followed immediately by a lower one as if to say, "I said 'why'?"

I stifled a giggle and Josh automatically shushed me. She heard it and let out three short, sharp whines, starting high and going down the scale, followed by a bash with her paw against the bars of the crate. I got out of bed and the moment she saw I was on my way over to her, her tail started thumping each side of the crate, another sound that would melt my heart each morning.

I slid open the front of the crate and she tumbled out and proceeded to say hello by frantically running around my ankles and jumping up to get closer to me, all the time doing her side to side dance as her tail took over the whole of her body.

I picked her up and, seeing as we had decided to try putting her toilet pad in the bathroom one more time, I took her straight in there and placed her on it. She looked at me as if to say, "Well, what have you brought me in here for?"

"Do a wee," I coaxed. She ignored me and walked around the bathroom, sniffing.

"Do a poo," I encouraged again. It was important to stay calm and be consistent so she didn't get stressed or confused, which would make the whole toilet training palaver a longer process. After ten long minutes and not even the slightest hint of a wee or poo obeying my commands, we found ourselves sitting opposite one another, having a staring competition. I decided not to make a big deal of it and left her to do her business in peace whilst I put the kettle on.

On days when we weren't working, Josh and I usually started the day by one of us making tea and bringing it back to bed. We liked to start the day slowly and sometimes we ended up chatting and then letting it extend to a second cup. *May as well keep up the routine we are used to*, I thought, so I opened the bathroom door, ready to slip through a small gap and close it behind me.

Leela was at the ready and the moment the door opened, she shot through my legs and scuttled into the living room. I knew where she was heading and acted quickly by snatching up the training pad and making a dash for the wealth corner. There she was, emptying her bladder with a satisfied look on her face. I squealed and tried to shove the pad under her. She looked startled and tried to move away from it. *Oh no*, I thought, *she'll end up being scared of the pad.*

"It's okay, do a wee, good girl, do a wee!" I sang, with sheer panic ringing through my voice. I clumsily picked her up mid wee and tried to place her on the pad. BIG mistake. She ran away from me and peed right across the floor and under the settee. I had to think quickly. Dogs get conditioned so easily that if I got this wrong, the whole flat could become a dog toilet!

I soaked up the wee with the pad and then praised it. "Good wee!" I gleefully shouted, hoping the neighbours were out. "What a good wee! Yes! Good wee!" I was improvising now. I looked under the settee and saw two little button eyes staring back at me, saying, "You're mad, I want to go home".

I continued to praise her and eventually her tail started wagging but she stayed put, obviously still suspicious. I decided to go back to plan A and put the kettle on and give her a chance to come out in her own time. I put a clean pad down next to the soiled one, hoping she would understand and then went into the kitchen, flicked the switch on the kettle and took a cloth into the living room to clean up the carpet. Leela was out from under the settee about a foot away from the clean toilet pad in the dreaded rounded spine position, doing the biggest poo that it was possible for a puppy to do!

I stopped the yelp rising from my throat just in time for it to turn into a strangled squeak and Leela looked straight at me, with fear in her eyes. She was clearly confused and thought she was doing wrong. She was, but now wasn't the time to tell her. I had obviously completely messed up with my communications. I put a big smile on my face and decided to explain later.

"Good girl, Leela!" I said joyfully. When she had finished, I used a plastic bag to put the poo on the pad and then made a big fuss.

"Good poo!" I squealed delightedly, now praying the neighbours weren't in. "Very good poo!"

Leela was oblivious to what I meant but nevertheless was delighted she had pleased me and enthusiastically accepted the praise and the treat. Puppies like to please you; they need to please you as their survival depends on fitting in well with the pack. I knew she didn't have a clue as to why she was getting the treat after the appalling way I had handled the whole incident, but at least she was no longer scared of me. I stood up, feeling a bit better about it all and headed for the kitchen.

I washed my hands, flicked the switch on the kettle again and took a bin bag out of the cupboard to put the pads in. I walked back into the living room to find that Leela had vomited the treat back onto to the carpet and was standing looking all pathetic and sorry for herself. My heart went out to her. I picked her up and sat on the settee, holding her close. She relaxed and snuggled into my chest and I sighed and smiled to myself. It was comforting to realise that I felt happy after a morning of cleaning up poo, wee and sick and at the same time desperately trying to figure out how to communicate the right thing to this tiny bundle of chaos! A sense of peace washed over me as I listened to the rhythmic sound of her breathing and felt her tiny body surrender what little weight she had into my arms. I thought about our usual harmonious, calm start to the day and it seemed cold and clinical next to this experience. It was good to be needed and good to be able to give what was needed. I had spent years looking for inner peace, only to find it in chaos!

I was getting cold. I had forgotten to put the heating on like I normally did when I woke up. I carried Leela to the kitchen and flicked the kettle on, determined that the fourth attempt to complete the task of making tea that morning would be a success.

As I opened the bedroom door to join Josh for our morning beverage in bed an hour later than planned, I saw him close his eyes quickly and pretend to be asleep. I knew his game. He had heard the commotion, couldn't be bothered to come and help, and had just listened to the whole thing instead. To avoid being in the doghouse, he was now pretending he had fallen innocently back into a deep sleep and heard nothing. The fact that I was deliriously happy didn't get in the way of me deciding to give him a hard time, anyway. I knew that it must have sounded hilarious to anyone listening, but I wasn't going to let him get away with shirking his responsibilities that easily.

I put his tea down silently on his side of the bed and tiptoed round to my side, allowing him to think I believed his fake slumber was the real thing and gently got back into bed. Leela was too small to get on the bed without help, but nevertheless she was determined, as she hurled herself at it again and again. I liked her spirit; she wasn't one to give up easily, unlike the person in the throes of an Oscar-wannabe performance next to me. I picked her up and dropped her onto Josh's head. When she realised where she had landed, she went into a frenzy of joy, licking his face, wagging her whole torso and stampeding all over his face and body.

Josh, meanwhile, continued to do some very bad 'I have just been jarred awake out a deep sleep where I couldn't possibly have heard any of the drama that has been going on in the other room' acting. I fixed my 'I don't believe you' glare on my face and stared at him. It took a few minutes of him trying to sit up and control Leela, whilst maintaining the pantomime startled look on his face. It was a poor effort to keep up the pretence of not realising I was staring at him. I carried on; he would have to meet my gaze at some point. He pummelled his pillows, sat back, arranged the bedclothes and, having run out of things to do, slowly let his eyes wander up the duvet to meet mine.

We looked at each other and I saw a number of different thoughts and plans pass through his eyes. *Should I just laugh...? No, be serious... Play dumb... Oh no, she knows. She's not happy... I'll just apologise... Shit!*

I watched him surrender any kind of escape plan and just look me squarely in the eyes, ready to take the blow. I paused; just one more moment of sweet revenge. Then we both collapsed into uncontrollable giggles. It was a great way to start the day.

Chapter Twenty-Four

THE LANGUAGE OF DOG

Later on that day, Josh set off to work in France. He would be away for seven days. It took a long time for him to say goodbye to Leela, as it was obviously hard for him to go. We were both enjoying that wonderful, warm feeling that surrounds you when something good has happened in life... the feeling that where you are is the only place you want to be. It's funny how often sadness can accompany these times. I guess, when you feel so expansive, it also gives room and strength for feelings that are not so easy to be with to surface. I felt so elated to have Leela at home, yet, at the same time, seeing Josh enjoy her so much and be so tender as he cuddled her goodbye, made me long to carry his child.

I stayed in for the first couple of days, only taking Leela out early in the mornings to Hove Lawns when it wasn't so busy, so she could get used to her neighbourhood slowly. The toilet training was going well now. I had turned a blind eye to what we may be encouraging more of in our wealth corner. My main concern was how she reacted when I put her in her crate and left her in the bedroom alone. The breeder had told me that Leela had been fine in her crate for a couple of hours whilst she went to work each day. However, when I tried it, she was quiet whilst I was still in the room – in fact, she quite happily went to bed in it every night knowing we were just a few feet away in our bed – but the moment I left the room, it was another story. She would whimper and cry, bash the bars with her paws and work herself into a howl.

Now, I know the intellectual advice is to leave them and let them cry it out but, when faced with a choice, I always veer to the side of instinct and, to leave anyone to cry and scream alone, let alone a ten-week-old puppy, went against every instinctual bone in my body. I just couldn't do it. I tried several times, but listening to her distress always ended up with me exhausted and in floods of tears. When she got that upset, I knew I had failed her in some way.

On day four of only going out to the beach or Hove Lawns with her, I reached a point where I had to go out and do some food shopping and, as food stores only allow guide dogs, I had to leave her alone at home. It was also important that I deal with her separation anxiety.

I put Leela in her crate and stroked her through the bars. She happily snuffled her wet nose into my palm whilst I explained to her that I was going out to the shops on a very busy road that would probably frighten her until she was more used to people and traffic and that no amount of crying was going to get her out of her crate. I would be away for a little while and then we could play again. Feeling confident she was secure enough, I stood up, walked out of the bedroom and closed the door.

After what seemed like ten long minutes of sitting outside listening to her howl, I could stand it no longer.

I got my coat on, put Leela inside it and marched down to the shops. Until I had found a way to do this, she would just have to stay with me. It felt lovely having her inside my coat, her little head popping out to have a nosy at the loud and busy city from the safety of my jacket. So many people's faces lit up when they noticed her. I hoped I'd see the same look from the supermarket staff at Waitrose. Unfortunately, their expressions didn't quite match the look of delight on the faces of the passers-by and we lasted about thirty seconds before we were walking out of the exit again. I considered going back with a white stick, but the thought of being dragged by an excited puppy through the supermarket at full pelt whilst having to keep my eyes shut, helped me decide not to rely on Leela's navigation skills just yet.

I walked back onto the street feeling anxious. How was I going to deal with this? She seemed relaxed and content enough to be with us, she had showed no signs of distress at leaving her first home, so why did she get so upset when I left her? My sisters hadn't had the same problems, although Kaye had two dogs that were always together so I suppose that made a difference. Maxine's dog, Cookie, seemed to have settled in well right from the start.

I decided to go to Waterstones and find a dog-training book. I wanted to find a natural way to communicate with her. I had spent a few years doing natural horsemanship and it made sense to me that we need to speak the language of the animal. I don't believe that forcing or 'breaking' an animal in constitutes a good relationship. An obedient one, yes, but not necessarily a happy one. Leela was enjoying herself, experiencing the world from the security of my jacket, her little curled-up body pressed into mine. Whenever a big truck or bus went by, I put my hand inside and stroked her chubby, warm belly to reassure her and every now and then she would stick her nose under my arm and have a snooze. She must have felt so cosy and safe.

I went straight up to the animal section and scoured through book after book, looking for some tips. *This is what a new mum must go through when her baby won't stop crying and she feels she is getting it all wrong*, I thought, at the same time deciding to keep that thought to myself. I wasn't a new mum, I was a new dog owner and I didn't want people looking at me sadly as I confused the two.

When the umpteenth book I picked up was still saying leave the puppy to cry, I was starting to feel desperate. No matter which expert was advising it, I knew it wasn't right. Neither did it fit in with the philosophy of natural horsemanship. Now, I am perfectly aware that a dog is a completely different animal from a horse. Dogs wag their tails and resent it when you sit on their backs and give them grass to eat and horses look at you with contempt when you ask them to sit and then offer them a bone. (I'm quite an expert, you know!) However, I was sure there was a more natural philosophy to follow when communicating with a dog.

Then, aha! A title of a book jumped out at me. *The Dog Listener*, by Jan Fennell. I pulled it off the shelf and flicked through. A few minutes gave me enough of an overview to realise that this was the method for me. Jan said that no matter how intelligent a dog is, it is our job to learn their language, not their job to learn ours and, it seemed that she was the woman that could teach me to do just that. I felt excited. I was about to be initiated into the language of Dog, which promised to help me develop a greater understanding and bond with man's best friend.

I paid for the book and hurried home to spend the whole night reading, with Leela curled up on my lap and the rain beating hard against the window. It was coming up to Christmas and cosy nights in were extra special with a fluffy puppy for company. As the evening progressed, it became clear where I was going wrong. The good news was that it wasn't too difficult to put right. Jan said that dogs have a simple etiquette and rules are few. If they aren't in place, however, it causes them to feel insecure and confused. I had tried to welcome Leela in the way a human would want to be welcomed. Big fuss in the morning when I first took her out of her crate and feeding her with us so she felt part of the family. However, according to Jan's observations and experience, this gives a dog very confused messages.

Like most natural philosophies, it made simple sense. In order to instil a feeling of security in your dog, it was important to let them know *you* were top dog and therefore in charge. Dogs at the bottom of the pack had the easiest life and were meant to enjoy being provided for, protected and guided when needed and be a welcome member of the community.

Four things were to be put in place in order for Leela to understand I was top dog.

1. I had to ignore her for at least five minutes after we had been separated. It seemed that, unlike me, top dog never goes bounding up to the pack saying, "Hi guys, really great to see you! Missed you so much, come and give Mummy a kiss, aw, I have missed

you," etc. etc. Instead, they command respect by keeping their distance, avoiding eye contact and being calm and confident, giving off the vibe to the pack that all is well. When top dog is ready and has full respect from the other members of the community, they will engage with the pack and be as loving and playful as the rest. Unlike me, they were never cajoled or guilt-led into playing a game.

2. I should always eat first and feed Leela second. Top dog will always feed first in the wild and then the rest eat what is left; a 'biggy' in the way of stating your rank. Being a vegetarian, I was relieved to read on and find out I didn't have to wrench chunks of meat apart and allow grease to drip down my chin in order to make the point. I simply had to put a cracker next to her bowl and make it look like I was taking it from her portion, eat it and then feed her.

3. I was to always lead the hunt! I was to go out of the door first to check for danger and not allow her to pull me down the road. She had to stay at my heel and trust I knew where I was going and what I was doing. I just hoped she would never understand the navigation arguments Josh and I would inevitably have in the future, as we circled a roundabout for the fifth time, getting nowhere, just shouting louder.

4. In times of perceived danger, I was to take the lead. So no more delighting guests by opening the door just enough to let a comical, chubby, furry friend greet them, whilst I beamed proudly on the other side, listening to squeals of delight from my friends as she slobbered all over them.

I went to bed that night feeling optimistic, fluent in the language of Dog and ready to start afresh.

The next morning, I spent the first few moments enjoying the little whimpers and indignant thwacks of her paws against the bar. Smiling and feeling your heart swell with affection must be the healthiest way to start any day. I eventually got up and, instead of peering through the bars and talking excitedly to her, I avoided eye contact, slid open the door and turned my back on her to walk to the kitchen. She paused a moment and then I heard her tumble out and follow me down the hall. I had to use every inch of willpower not to pick her up when I felt her tiny front paws jumping up my leg to get my attention. I loved it when she was warm and clumsy with sleep and in need of a cuddle. Instead, I followed Jan's instructions, kept avoiding eye contact but gently put my hand on her chest and guided her down; she jumped up again so I repeated the physical instruction. Making any verbal sound was equivalent to giving her attention so it was important to do everything silently.

As I filled the kettle, I could see her out of the corner of my eye. She was standing still, apart from her wagging tail, and was weighing me up. I was delighted when she did exactly what it said in the book and lay down. This meant she was relaxed and knew I was in charge. It was a wonderful feeling and at the same time I could see how people would naturally interpret this as the dog being upset at being ignored. She wasn't; she was content and, more importantly, respecting my space, which is the privilege of top dog.

After I made my tea, I continued to practice my new language skill by cutting a small piece of cheese for her, crouching down and calling her to me. She came and took the cheese; this was my way of saying that I provided for her. I stroked her neck and she happily trotted off to the toilet. I was amazed at how easy it was to calm her down. I must admit I missed our usual greeting, but it felt much more important to give her the right message. And, now I had met with her in the way she understood, I could play and rough and tumble with her as much as I liked.

The next test was the crate. I waited a couple of hours and did rule No. 2, which was to pretend to eat some of her food before I gave it to her. Then, when I was ready, I confidently walked into the bedroom, knowing she would follow. Dogs, like horses, sense your intent so there was no point in picking her up nervously, hoping she wasn't going to kick off the moment I walked out of the bedroom. Neither was there any point in pretending; they sniff out pretence, so it's what you mean, not what you say, that's important. I had to be absolutely confident that she was going to be happy in there for the duration and that it was me who was making the decisions around here. Once in the bedroom, I picked her up and placed her firmly in the crate. She was still weighing it all up. She knew something had radically changed today and she was on the alert and ready to mark my exam papers. "So, you think you can talk Dog, then?" she was saying. "Well, I think I will be the judge of that!"

Still avoiding eye contact, I closed the door of the crate and walked out of the bedroom, closing the door firmly behind me and then waited in anticipation. A little whimper and then silence. Another whimper followed by a bash of the paw. Shit, this is how it always started.

Soon she would be howling. A louder whimper and a stronger bash got the better of me. This could not go on.

I opened the door, pointed my finger at her and shouted,

"Leela! Stop it!" and quickly shut the door again. I wasn't sure that that was part of the rulebook but, if things went on like this, we couldn't keep her. How could we live our lives if we had to be with her 24/7? We would have to get a dog nanny! I don't believe any dog should be left on its own all day, every day and our intention was to have her with us most of the time, but we had to be able to leave her sometimes.

I stood in the corridor and held my breath. Complete silence. It dawned on me that she had picked up on my intention just then; I really had meant what I had said. I guess I was tense with anticipation when I left the bedroom the first time and Leela had responded to that. Jan Fennell said that if they think that they are in charge, they will get distressed when you leave them and panic that you are going out into the big, wide world without their protection. It isn't that they feel insecure without *us*, they get distressed because they can't take care of us when they have been given the position of top dog. That made perfect sense and I had communicated clearly to her this morning that I had promoted myself overnight and was now the boss. I think the intention behind what I had just shouted at her had finally let the news sink in. I was in charge; her job was to chill out and enjoy herself.

Twenty minutes later, I went into the bedroom, slid open the crate and ignored her for five minutes before giving her a treat and playing with her. I repeated this procedure three times that day and by the third time, she happily clambered in to her crate and lay down and went to sleep even before I had reached the bedroom door. This time, I also opened and slammed the front door to give her the impression I had actually left the flat. Not a peep out of her. The message had been received and I was officially top dog! I swaggered down the hallway and poured myself a celebratory glass of wine. I was bloody brilliant. Eat your heart out, Dr Doolittle!

Chapter Twenty-Five

A SPOKE IN THE WHEEL

When Josh got back, I proudly initiated him into the new language and he was amazed at how quickly Leela responded to him. It felt so much better to be in charge. Leela was now happy to be alone in her crate occasionally and, because she trusted us, this also meant she was safer, as she respected our instructions to stay close or come to us when we needed her to.

Next, we looked at diet and health. Seeing as both Josh and I opt for a natural approach, we wanted to do the same with Leela. I began researching information on natural dog care and, came across a holistic vet practising in a village called East Hoathly, about ten miles out of Brighton. It was good to get a different angle on health care and information on how to deal with fleas, worms, vaccines and other ailments naturally, rather than bombarding her body with chemicals. After visiting the vet, who seemed very balanced in his view, and after reading various books and articles, we decided to do one lot of regular vaccines and then boost her every year homoeopathically. We would worm her with herbs and keep her coat flea-free by using a spray of garlic and lavender, as well as boosting her diet with garlic.

Diet was another mind-boggling area. Again, we opted for a more natural approach of raw bones, organic meat and raw vegetables and a bag of dry dog food with no additives for times when we needed to make life easy. I wasn't over-keen on handling meat as so far, I had always asked even my meat-eating friends to keep my home vegetarian. It was clear from our research, though, that dogs need bones and meat to be healthy. Josh didn't have any qualms about handling meat having worked as a chef for so many years. I, on the other hand, found it hard to even go into the meat section of a supermarket so I had a bit of a phobia to face.

Education and lifestyle decided on, we got down to the business of being a family of three, which meant having lots of fun. It was still a time of trial and error and remembering to keep up the good habits of speaking Dog to her, rather than expecting her to mould into the complex world of human relationships. It was amazing to see how, if I failed to fulfil my role as top dog, she would soon let me know she didn't trust me as a leader simply by refusing to follow me, therefore making me redundant. Oh, how logical and obvious. If only our political system could be as straightforward!

I soon learned that I had to mean what I said and be consistent in order to keep her respect and trust. So many times I asked for something without conviction, or without really expecting her to co-operate, and so many times she co-operated with my expectation rather than my command. She was my teacher, constantly showing me when my words, thoughts and intentions weren't aligned.

There is one particular incident that stands out. I had been a bit lax with the 'five minute rule' of ignoring her when we had been separated. I had also turned a blind eye a few times when she jumped on furniture without permission. Boundaries and territory are really important ways of communication and although she was allowed on the bed and furniture, she had to wait for our permission, in order to be clear whose space she was in. I had let this rule slip a few times and, as a consequence, she had been testing the boundaries.

On this particular morning, she had pulled on the lead all the way to the beach and I had let her ignore my protests. When I set her free, she ran ahead like she normally did and I waited a few moments before changing direction. She didn't follow me as she should and after a few minutes, I got worried I would lose her. I then did the big 'no-no' of turning back and walking towards her, all the while calling her to me and getting more and more frustrated. She picked up on my fear of not being able to control her and stayed just out of reach. She was thoroughly enjoying the game and thoroughly in charge.

Eventually, I sat down on the stony beach and admitted failure. She mooched about, a few feet away from me and then picked something up. As she trotted past me, I realised that she had a beer can in her mouth and the top of it had been sliced, leaving a razor-sharp edge that could do a lot of damage to her delicate mouth. I had to get it off her.

"Leave it!" I heard myself say, with a determination that shot through the whole of my body. Leela froze mid-trot, the conviction in my voice having made her pay attention.

"Leave it!" I repeated, fully focused on the task. It wasn't fear I felt, just that there was no option; she had to drop that can. Very gently, she lowered her head and released it from her mouth.

"Come here," I said, with the same expectation. She came straight to me and I put her lead on, before retrieving the can to put it safely in the bin. Leela trotted beside me in silence all the way home and didn't pull once.

I felt totally in awe of what had just happened. I kept going over the incident so I could remember how it felt when I really got behind what I said. Although I had often changed situations around through sheer determination, it wasn't always consistent and I was also capable of exhausting myself by letting my mind swing from feeling focused and confident, to fear and doubt, which no doubt also changed the outcome of events. I felt that an ancient secret had been revealed to me that day.

Having somewhere to express my maternal instincts also helped me to relax about getting pregnant. Although Leela was a different kind of dependant, she was still a dependant and made us three, rather than two. It was lovely to see her toys dotted around the flat; a bit of chaos made it more homely and cosy. Call it wishful thinking – and most people who knew that I was forty-three and Josh was fifty-one did – I still had the feeling that when the time was right, I would become pregnant and after the can incident with Leela, I knew it was even more important not to let any shadow of doubt interfere with this feeling.

The experience with Leela had shown us that we were well and truly ready to give up our so-called freedom and embrace a different lifestyle. Although having Leela, especially in the first few months of settling her in, meant that I could no longer stay at parties as long as I wanted, or spend long afternoons with friends in cafés where dogs weren't allowed, or just go off for the day on my own, I never felt restricted by her. The richness, fun and depth of feeling she had brought with her from the moment she had stumbled out of the kitchen door in Worcester, far outweighed having the extra responsibility. We both agreed on this and surprised ourselves with how easy we found it. Being used to doing exactly what we wanted when we wanted, at the drop of a hat, we had expected to feel that our freedom had been curtailed, but instead, we felt a contentment and connection that we had never experienced before. She had taught us a new meaning of freedom.

By the beginning of January, Leela was completely settled, and house-trained to sit at the door when she needed to go to the loo. Work had started to come in, which meant being away from home more often and Leela stayed with a number of eager friends, who were more than happy to oblige when we needed help. I didn't like leaving Leela and was finding that more and more, I wanted to stay home. I saw this as a good sign that I was again giving out the right signals and was ready to commit to being a mum. Very soon, the little soul who had chosen us as Mum and Dad would take the plunge and join us. I wished it were more viable to give up work and stay home to look after a dog, but, try as I did, I couldn't quite justify it. I talked over my feelings with Josh and we both came to the conclusion that waiting for a baby as an excuse to change our lifestyle was not healthy; we needed to make some changes now.

The work we had the most flexibility with was also the most frequent job at that time and one that took us away to France for three days in a row. It was a corporate course that had been running continuously for over a year and was set to run for another six months. We specialised in the health and well-being section and Josh and I shared the same role of teaching Energy Management, which meant taking it in turns to go to France and deliver the programme. As Josh was really enjoying the work and the travel, he offered to take on my commitments as that way, I could focus on working from home. Our plan for when we had a family was to design and deliver our own retreats and workshops so we had more independence and choice about where and when we worked. Why not start to create that now? Surely that would take us closer to our dream life? It would also give me a job to do and a reason to stay at home more. So it was settled. By the end of January, Josh took over my bookings in France and I focused on creating a new career path for us.

I loved my new role and being at home with Leela. I felt closer than ever to becoming a mum and creating the life that would suit a family. I continued to use energy medicine techniques to help me conceive and I also continued to see Jonathan Hutson the cranial osteopath and Sarah Arden the reflexologist to help boost my fertility;. Although I saw them completely independently of each other, they both confirmed what I myself was beginning to feel – a new surge of strength in my energies and being closer to conceiving a child.

I haven't left many stones unturned on my road of self-development and my search for good health. I have met some amazing practitioners, healers and wise people, some very scientific and logical in their approaches and some extremely quirky, with way-out beliefs. How people know what they know and do what they do isn't so important to me. However, I have developed discernment around who and what I will engage with. Jonathan and Sarah are very different in their approaches. Jonathan is very down to earth, chooses his words carefully and his practice is gentle. Sarah, on the other hand, is extremely colourful and enthusiastic both in word and deed and indeed has had me pulling my foot away from her strong hands on many an occasion with a yelp, as she seized on an energy blockage with gusto. What the two of them have in common is compassion, wisdom and the ability to help and empower at the same time. The fact that their observations tallied time and time again, was proof enough for me that the fertility procedures that the medical industry had to offer were not necessary for me.

I saw Sara for reflexology mid-January 2008 and she asked me if I would be interested in doing a ritual to help me conceive. I agreed to give it a try and she responded by giving me a photocopy from a page of a book and some instructions. I was to copy a letter out in an ancient language. The letter was to the angel St Germaine, asking for any remaining obstruction that may be preventing me from conceiving to be removed. I was to do it on a Saturday using a white pen on black paper and then bury it in a public place. In for a penny, in for a pound, I thought and tucked it into my bag. Sara gave me her wide and always ready smile.

"I've had incredible results using this. You're ready for it now," she said, with a twinkle in her eye.

I read the photocopy when I got home, which explained that this was an old ritual and had to be respected. Anyone participating in this ritual should be prepared to have their life turned upside down if necessary, in order for their wish to be fulfilled. Mmmm… I paused a moment at that one, but then, after a short while, decided that I actually *wanted* my life turned upside down. I was ready for a shake-up and it felt exciting to tempt fate. So, on the Saturday morning, I got up and carefully copied out the beautiful signs and shapes that made up my letter to St Germaine.

Josh stood silently by and watched over my shoulder. He trusted Sarah as much as I did and, although this felt bonkers, we were both willing to push aside any cynicism and give it a try. After I had finished, we folded it carefully and walked in silence to St Anne's Wells Gardens, one of our favourite parks in Hove. Needless to say, there was also a hint of expectation that some reality TV host was about to appear and shame us on national TV for being so gullible.

Once in the park, we chose a pretty corner in the nature reserve section and ceremoniously buried our letter, hearts filled with hope that this was the final frontier. I stared at the ground, wondering how on earth this would make a difference to our lives and also enjoying the surge of confidence that swept through me, assuring me that it would. This was raw magic in the making. Our culture is now pretty much devoid of meaningful ritual, and magic has become a fluffy word to be scorned or, at most, feared. Before the rise of power over people and profit above all, before God became a separate entity that was to be feared, pleased and obeyed, ritual and magic were commonplace and a natural way to connect with the earth and acknowledge that we are powerful co-creators of life and the help of a loving intelligence far greater than us was available to anyone who chose to commune.

"Fancy a fry-up?" Josh said, bringing me fully back to earth.

"Thought you'd never ask." We linked arms and walked out of the park gates. It would be a good year before we would remember this ritual and talk about it again.

Give or take a few days, I was usually like clockwork with my period and for the last three or four years, that time of the month was tense, to say the least. I would wake up on the day I was due and spend the morning convinced I was pregnant. I would try to remember what time I had started the month before and convince myself it was a few hours earlier, and begin to feel more and more pregnant as the minutes went by. These days were torturous, as I would swing from being so convinced and excited, to being calm and logical. I would get the pregnancy-testing kit out a dozen times and then be too scared to be disappointed and talk myself into waiting another day.

On the months I did do a test, it was after working myself up so much that I was absolutely convinced that I was pregnant. I would snatch the test out of the bathroom cabinet before I had a chance to change my mind again, pee on the stick and then sit staring at the two little windows. A line would show up in the control window telling me I had done the test correctly. Now, all I needed was for the other window to produce a cross, showing a positive result; a single line would mean negative. The two minutes of waiting for the stick to process the result seemed like hours and I hallucinated that a faint cross was appearing so many times, I would rub my eyes and tilt the stick, willing it to get stronger. Eventually, with a sickening build-up in my throat and pushing back tears full of anger and disappointment, I would stare at the one line that was screaming out my failure.

What always followed was a complete reframing of how I was experiencing time. Suddenly, half a day – or a day, if I had managed to stretch it that long – didn't seem like a long time to be late at all and I would feel so stupid for allowing myself to have had all that hope. Before the test, even an hour seemed like an age. I would even be looking at my stomach to see if it was swollen and convincing myself I felt nauseous. The moment I knew I wasn't pregnant, it seemed unbelievable that I could have been so gullible and my behaviour seemed ridiculous and totally neurotic. What a waste of time, energy and money even considering I could be pregnant. Next time, I would wait at least a week before even considering doing a test. It was usually only a matter of hours, or, at the longest, the next day, before my period would rub salt into my wounds with its arrival.

Towards the end of January, I went through the whole process again. I was three-quarters of a day late and absolutely sure that, with all the changes plus the ritual, there was nothing holding us back. Nevertheless, once more I sat there staring at the plastic stick in despair as it told me I was not pregnant. Only this month it was different, because my period never came; not the next day, the day after, or the day after that. By this time, I had done three further tests, all three of which gave the same negative result as the first. I felt cheated and angry. What was going on? I spent hours trawling the internet for stories of people who had the same experiences as me and had then found they were pregnant. No luck, just a few nutters who hadn't read the instructions properly.

After the fifth test a week later, I decided to ignore what was going on. Maybe I was more stressed than I realised. Maybe I would just miss a month, as something amazing was happening to my body and I was preparing to conceive!

About three weeks later, I woke up in the middle of the night drenched with sweat. I kicked off the duvet in a panic and lay naked, enjoying the freezing cold air on my skin. Two minutes later, I was freezing cold and grabbing the duvet again. This went on night after night and I began to feel panic rising each time it happened. My body was changing. The sweats began to creep into the day. In a flash, I would be bright red in the face and sweating, rushing to get my jumper off only to be hurriedly putting it back on again as my temperature plummeted only minutes later. It was a good month and several pregnancy tests later before I acknowledged sadly to myself that these were symptoms of the menopause.

I finally plucked up the courage to go and see Jonathan for a cranial treatment, expecting him to tell me the worst. After a quiet treatment that lulled me into a dreamlike state, he announced that he wasn't sure why my periods had stopped but my hypothalamus was not showing the usual signs of change and he was convinced that I was not menopausal. He still felt there was nothing to stop me becoming pregnant.

A few days later, I booked a session with Sarah. Surely this was the point where they would disagree? As usual, I refrained from mentioning any of Jonathan's most recent observations and was surprised once again when, mid-treatment, she said, "Your hypothalamus is definitely not reflecting any menopausal signs and I do feel that, spiritually, you are pregnant. I know there is a soul around you, so it is only a matter of time before you become pregnant."

As much as I tried to find comfort in what Sarah and Jonathan had told me, this had been going on for too long now. Five years too long, in fact. It was becoming increasingly difficult to remain positive and, for the first time in my life, I felt old. I have never really taken much notice of age and felt that people hung too much importance on it. I have always had the opinion that you should do things when you are ready to and not let your age, or more importantly other people's opinions about your age, dictate how you behave or what you do with your life. However, the thought that I was now moving into a new stage of my life before I was ready, gave rise to a whole cascade of confusing feelings.

I had always envisaged myself embracing and celebrating my menopause. I didn't like how it was viewed in our culture, another mystery of life that is controlled and hidden rather than celebrated. Something to be annoyed about, or ashamed of, instead of a stage of life to be embraced and enjoyed. There is a surge of wisdom and power that accompanies the menopause, a time for a woman to leave behind her childbearing years and become a wise and valued member of the community. It's a power lost in a sea of negativity that we have created through buying into the ridiculous notion that youth should be celebrated and aging condemned; that the unruly emotional cycle of a woman and her bodily functions should be controlled through medicine, or dampened down through our patriarchal beliefs that intellect should overrule instinct and emotion. I wanted to embrace this stage of my life, but not yet! I hadn't experienced the childbearing part yet and I felt cheated and betrayed by my own body. Why was it doing this to me at forty-three?

Yet it seemed I had no choice but to put that part of my life on hold. I couldn't even think about being a mum without a hot sweat coming on. They were like ghostly threats waiting in the wings to shadow all hope. Neither was I ready to give up the dream yet, so I decided to block it out for the time being and enjoy what I had with Leela and my new lifestyle. I really relied on her company and wisdom in those difficult months and she was always there, bursting with enthusiasm and love.

Josh was equally supportive. He wasn't ready to let go of the dream yet, either and we came to an agreement not to talk about it, at least for a while and let nature take its course.

March, April and May came and there was still no sign of my body supporting our dreams. Something kept urging me to make a big move. I woke up so many times with a sense of urgency to pack up and go somewhere else. Getting Leela and changing our work pattern clearly wasn't enough; we needed to do something else. Yet I didn't see the sense in just packing up and leaving for the sake of it. I was willing to follow my instinct, but I needed a little more guidance before doing something so irrational.

It was the end of May when Leela, no doubt fed up with me navel-gazing and asking for clearer guidance as to what to do next, decided to take matters into her own paws.

Our 'sign' came in the form of a letter from the landlord. In short, it read: *It has come to our attention that you have a dog in the flat. This dog has fouled in the public hallway, which is unfair and unacceptable to the other residents in the building. We ask that the dog be removed immediately.*

That was it. Not a bolt of lightning or job offer in sight, just the dog peeing on the carpet and pissing the landlord off!

As I read the letter, I felt something I had experienced only once before in my life. It was the moment I got sacked from that job teaching aerobics that I both hated and depended upon. A sinking feeling of 'Oh no!' and alongside it, a rising excitement saying, 'Oh yes!' Things were about to change. It had finally happened, the push we had been waiting for. 'Removing' Leela was out of the question. If she had to go, we all had to go!

I knew the 'fouling' he was talking about. About three weeks back, the boiler had broken and we had one of the landlord's workmen around to fix it. It was bizarre really, because we had had Leela for five months by then and she was perfectly house-trained. However, on the day Steve came round with the boiler man and I opened the door to let him in, Leela uncharacteristically pushed through my legs, ran out into the hallway and peed on the carpet. Surprised and embarrassed, I bustled Steve in the door and through to the kitchen where the boiler was and ran back to clean up the mess, hoping he hadn't noticed. Obviously he had, and had felt it was his duty to inform the landlord.

The more I thought about the incident, the more excited I felt about how this was absolutely meant to be. Leela had done this on purpose! She had seized the moment that was to change our lives; it was pure magic in action. The experience of the miracle wrapped in the mundane also allowed me to override any feelings of disdain for Steve, who had basically grassed on us and, in the process, done us a favour. We had no choice now, we had to move! In fact, I felt generous enough to feel grateful to Steve and his part in the great web of life. Wow! Move over, Mother Theresa, not only was I getting help from the Good Lord Above in the form of pee stains on the carpet, I was also filled with understanding and compassion!

The letter from the landlord was obviously a call to adventure and, although we knew that we could probably have smoothed things over with him – after all, we had been good tenants for over ten years – we also knew that, if we didn't take this opportunity, we could end up staying another ten years waiting for a stronger sign to move.

There is an old story about a man who stood on the roof of his house in a flood and called upon God to rescue him. As the waters rose around him, a raft came by and the people on it threw him a rope so he could join them. The man declined, telling them not to fear, God would save him. A little while later, the water was around his ankles and a boat came by. The people on the boat called out to him to swim to them so they could pull him to safety. Again, secure in his faith that God would hear his prayers and come to save him, the man declined. As the water rose faster and reached his waist and then his chest, the man continued to pray and as the water reached his neck, a helicopter flew by and dropped a ladder down for him to climb. The man declined once again and a few minutes later, he drowned.

After reaching heaven he went to God, feeling angry and rejected and asked why, after his faith was so strong, was he not saved? God's reply was simple: "I sent you a raft, a boat and a helicopter. What more did you want?"

We realised that, as mundane and unromantic as it was, this was the rescue party calling and we could either decline or jump. Unlike the story, at first there was no obvious vessel to jump into for safety, but we decided to take the plunge, anyway. It was only after we had handed our notice in that it became obvious what our next move should be. As it happened, only a month before we had sold our old and untrustworthy VW camper, Rainbow, and bought a much newer model. It was hard to let Rainbow go as we had travelled far and wide in her throughout Europe and England and had many wonderful memories attached to her. We had decorated the interior with bright colours, the kitchen area had a homely country feel with sackcloth curtains, stone-effect tile worktop and a dainty little spice rack. The sleeping area was deep purple and turquoise, which felt cosy and warm. We loved Rainbow, but had thrown quite a lot of money at her in recent years and it was time to say goodbye and upgrade.

After selling her to a good home, we spotted a Peugot boxer in the auto trader and travelled up to the Lake

District to get her. This van was the complete opposite to Rainbow. New, factory-fitted interior, power steering, quiet engine and snazzy blinds that also turned into fly screens. She was lovely, but needed a bit of character putting into her. So far, all we had added was a spice rack. The spice rack in Rainbow was what had swung it for me when we first went to see her. It was so tiny and perfectly formed, it took me back to the Wendy house I'd had as a child and allowed me to overlook any misgivings her engine seemed to have! It was a selling point that somehow didn't blind Josh in quite the same way and there were quite a few stern discussions on what was really important.

We put a wood-effect lino floor over the carpet to make it more dog-friendly and added a few silk flowers, stickers and decorative things here and there, along with a little shrine on the dashboard. To complete the ritual of making her well and truly ours, we had a short ceremony and named her Romany. We had made plans to go off around England for the summer, do a few festivals and check out some new places. It didn't take long to reach the decision that we would extend our trip to indefinite and make Romany our home.

"It just feels right, doesn't it?" I said, as I let the envelope containing our notice fall into the post box.

"I guess so," said Josh

That was as far as we went in trying to make sense of it. It felt like a flow had just started and we knew it was important to act before we could reason ourselves out of it. Which was how we ended up spending a long and smelly night in a pub car park and how Leela and I ended up at Sally's, grateful (or not) for hot water and a bath.

Chapter Twenty-Six

PASSING TIME AT SALLY'S

July 2008

Sally had left for work when I woke the next morning. After indulging in a long practice that blew away all the cobwebs, I took Leela to the local park. Queens Park isn't the best place for dog walking, as although it's pretty and big, the dog area is ridiculously small. I dug my hands in my pockets and started to wander around the path. It was still damp and cloudy.

Easy-to-please Leela bounded into the park as if it was the best place she had ever visited. After a quick scout around, she spotted a Jack Russell and made a beeline for him, intent on nicking the ball he was happily playing with. He spotted the enemy in time and snatched it up, clamping it tightly in his jaws. His tail was still wagging and he had mischief in his eyes. She bounced right up to his face and they stood nose to nose for a few seconds, sniffing each other's faces before moving on to sniff bits you would slap a well-known friend for going near, let alone a stranger.

Dogs don't have private parts, just parts. It's all the same to them, and all perfectly socially acceptable.

I thought about our social etiquette and how we judge and label certain body parts, making them wrong somehow, yet at the same time we are obsessed and glamourise them. Dogs just enjoy them freely for what they are and we make multi-million pound industries out of ours. Seems bizarre that it's illegal to show them in public and yet perfectly acceptable to look at pictures of them in magazines, dressed up in lace and leather. What a complex breed we are! Even though I don't think I am quite ready to lead the way in encouraging my fellow humans to abandon their inhibitions and claim their birthright to liberate their genitals, I do think dogs have a much better attitude towards their private parts.

After they had checked each other out, they began to run around each other, sniffing, wagging tails, egging each other on with the ball and having their own little doggy conversation.

"All right? Not seen you here before."

"Only second time for me, great, isn't it? Just been in the bushes, they're fantastic!"

"Yeah, brilliant."

"Is that your dad sitting by the tree?"

"Yeah. That your mum walking towards us?"

"Yeah," sniff-sniff, wag-wag, "what's she like?"

"Pretty good really, bit grumpy in the mornings but you know, mustn't grumble. What about yours?"

"Not bad, bit on the dramatic side but no real worries."

"Mind if I ask you something?"

"No, go ahead"

"Does she pick your poo up?"

"Yes!"

"And put it in a bag?"

"Yes! And sometimes carries it around with her before putting it in this bin thing. Odd, isn't it?"

"Odd? Bloody unbelievable, if you ask me! I got called disgusting for scratching my ears near the dinner table the other night, Disgusting, I thought? Me? And you pick my poo up?"

"Weird, innit? Anyway must dash, see ya!"

"Oi!"

"What?"

"That's my ball."

"Tough, see ya!"

I called Leela over and insisted that she drop the ball. As I threw it to the Jack Russell, I smiled at him and said hello. He caught the ball and glanced at the empty poo bag hanging out of my pocket. I blushed and quickly pushed it back in. I turned my back on him and ordered my mind to behave itself.

Leela was now leaping across the green to check out another possible canine companion. The basset hound snapped at her, so she turned around and happily headed in the opposite direction. She never gave any energy to unpleasant experiences. Too busy looking for fun. In front of us, I could see an overweight boxer doing her best to keep up with her owner. Leela caught up and ran around in circles, dropping into play stance and trying to tease the young spirit out of her. I imagined their conversation...

"What's your name?"

"Leela... . . yours?"

"Jeanette."

"Oh."

"Does your mum pick your poo up?"

"Yes. Weird, isn't it?"

"Do you know why?"

"No, do you?"

"No, but it's not right, is it?"

"Oops, gotta go, my owner's kept walking, she won't look back now, just expect me to catch up. She's been reading *The Dog Listener*."

"Oh no, not *The Dog Listener*! I had to play dead in Waterstones last week to stop Deidre buying that."

"Really?"

"Yeah. Saw a border collie do it on a film last week, brilliant actor, got shot and threw himself on the ground all glassy-eyed, really convincing. Saw him on *Good Morning TV* the next day, healthy as a butcher. When I saw Deidre pick up that meddling book, I just copied him, threw meself at her feet and whimpered. Worked a treat. She panicked, dropped the book and carried me all the way home."

"Wow, that's clever, I'd never get away with that."

"Got hot milk and biscuits and lay on the settee with me own pillow and everything. She even put *Emmerdale* on for me."

"That's amazing! Not fair, really. I have to ask permission before I go on any furniture. Oops, blimey, my mum's miles away. Better dash. See ya!"

I could hear Leela thundering up behind me. I love that sound. I knew that if I turned around now, I'd see her going at full pelt, back legs almost going too fast for her front ones, ears flapping, mouth open as if she was roaring with laughter. I resisted the urge to turn and catch her in her element. I had walked away in the confidence that she would follow. She had taken her time and it was important to let her know that it was her responsibility to keep up with me. That way, we would never lose each other. She circled around me, letting me know she was back,

"Good girl, Leela!"

We followed the path around the kids' area and headed back for the park gates. As we got close to the road, I called Leela to me so I could put her lead on. She came straight away, she always did. I never had any trouble with her nowadays. I liked to think although Leela may complain about me a bit, she was secretly proud that her mum could speak 'the language' and was a real pack leader. My suspicions were confirmed as we left the park. I saw her draw herself up to her full height and smile smugly at a disgruntled-looking Chihuahua sitting on a bench. Next to her was her owner, smiling vaguely into space. They were wearing matching neckerchiefs and leather jackets.

I spent the afternoon staring out of the window watching the rain, with Leela curled up next to me fast asleep. It had really struck me in the last few days how habituated I had become. At one time, I would have made the move to get a dog, change my lifestyle or move on from where I was living much more quickly than it had taken me in more recent years. I would have recognised when it was time to try something new and done so without a backward glance. Admittedly, sometimes this decision would be fear-based, avoiding commitment or running away from being conventional, but also it had satisfied my love of fluidity and change, a need to explore life instead of settling for the familiar.

There is a downside to familiarity that can convince you that even though the situation may not be completely fulfilling, or even happy, it is still a better situation to be in because it's known and safe and therefore worth staying in. It's easy to stop learning, exploring and let life become habitual and new experiences seem threatening. It was clear now that although on the outside my life had seemed variable, with lots of travel and diverse work, I had actually fallen into a pretty predictable routine, playing safe and doing stuff I knew well, which led to the same kind of experiences year in, year out. The call to adventure had come around frequently, periodically giving me that restless feeling to go exploring and do something new and fresh, but I was too comfortable where I was and I had convinced myself that life had got as good as it could be, and, I should hang onto everything I had and not rock the boat. Going on safari and getting Leela had rekindled my curiosity and love of new experiences. It felt good to be in that zone again, although a tiny part of me was still looking back to see if my comfy slippers were still waiting for me under the bed.

I was still lost in thought when Sally came home from work.

"Good day?" she sang, as she breezed into the kitchen and Leela dived off the settee to greet her. "Hello, lovely puppy! Did you go to the park?"

It took me a while to come out of my pensive state and realise Leela wasn't going to answer her.

"Yeah, we had a wander down there and then had a cosy afternoon in. Good day at school?"

"Yes, got a lovely class of kids at the moment, been trying out my brain gym exercises and they are working a treat."

We had an early dinner and in the evening went to Sally's gig. She had recently started singing in a

Retro-country and western band. I was keen to see her but also wanted to avoid bumping into friends. I wasn't in the mood to be with lots of people. I wanted to be quiet for a few days and integrate the move.

I waited until ten minutes before Sally was due on stage and called a cab to take me to the pub, that happened to be just around the corner from Norfolk Square. The cab driver arrived and we set off to the seafront. As we drove past the West Pier, I toyed with the idea of asking him not to turn into Norfolk Square, which was the most obvious route, but as we got closer, curiosity got the better of me and I wanted to see how I felt, now I had been away a few days. We turned into Western Street and I craned my head to see the flat. It was dark, curtains open, nets drawn, looking chillingly empty. I felt no desire to rush back but I did feel a little sad. I hoped there would be someone nice in there soon to make it the home it deserved to be.

I slunk into the pub keeping my head down, ordered a glass of wine from the bar and hid at the back like some B-list celebrity. I didn't look around to see who else was there, I just fixed my eyes on the stage. The Righteous Ones were about to begin. Sally stood centre stage and looked a little nervous. This was only their fourth gig and singing in public was a new thing for her. I felt my stomach tighten with anxiety. Waiting for a performance to start, especially if it involves someone I know, always brings back the feeling of being in an audition that is going badly.

However, I needn't have worried for, after a slightly shy start, she warmed up and her voice got stronger and stronger. The knot in my stomach loosened. She was good. In fact, she was really good. I took a deep breath, and felt the tension drain away. The pub was nice and dark, the wine was good quality and the band were going down well. I leaned back in my chair, enjoying the rest of the performance and feeling content with life.

We passed the flat again on the way back, still dark and empty. I imagined going in and seeing it as it was, with all our furniture in place and climbing into bed. Fond as the memory was, I really didn't want to go back to it. Even though I knew the hardest bit was always before the change, I had still exhausted myself with 'what ifs' in the weeks we were preparing to leave. Now that we were over the threshold, it felt easy to let go and move forward.

Josh called when we got back. He was really enjoying the course but was also feeling a little out of sorts and looking forward to us all being together again. I finished the call feeling we were lucky to have each other.

I climbed into bed early. Leela flopped down beside me and gave one of her enormous sighs. I watched her sleep for a while, absolutely at peace with herself. A deeply restful, guiltless, shameless, worry-less sleep, her little white nose tucked into her jet-black body. I loved her so much. I curled my body around hers and, enjoying the stillness radiating from her, I let my mind and body join her in slumber land.

Chapter Twenty-Seven

THE GOOD LIFE

It was Sunday and Josh was on his way to pick us up from Sally's. Today, we were heading for Oxon Hoath as we had been booked along with our friend and colleague Jack to run a Well-Being programme for a literary company.

We kissed and licked our goodbyes to Sally (I'll leave it to you to decipher who did what!) and arranged to meet at One World Camp, where we were to play with the Maracatu band and, when Josh pulled up in Romany, we jumped in as quickly and eagerly as we had jumped out four days before.

A few hours later, we got off the main road and onto the leafy country lanes that led to the estate.

"Hello trees! Lovely to be back!" It was my ritual to say this as the first trees of the land waved their branches to greet us. I loved this place.

"Hiya!" Josh mimicked, in a high-pitched Mancunian accent. He did this every time and although it isn't that funny, it always makes us laugh. "Are yer all right? 'Ow ya bin?" he added.

I retaliated by tapping Ganesh in an over-earnest manner and sitting in the lotus position with a goofy look on my face.

We turned right, past the little gatekeeper's cottage onto a wide gravel path. A big space of rolling fields came into view. Leela sat alert, her body stiff with anticipation, ready to spring into action as she stared at the expanse of space in front of her. Usually, at this point I would open the door and we would watch her fly across the field at full pelt, breaking her thundering pace only to leap gleefully two or three times like a young deer before picking up speed again. It was a pure joy to watch. Today however, we wanted to get parked and the awning up before the weather broke. Nevertheless, Leela's nose stayed glued to the window in hope until we turned into the main driveway and past the Dower house. We ignored the main entrance and went all the way around to the back of the house to find our secret hideout.

We parked up, making sure we were well hidden from the house and opened the door. Leela shot out into the grounds to explore. She loved it here as much as we did, although she was equally excited about Queens Park or some tiny bit of garden. Our hideout was a small area to the side of the rose garden situated at the east side of the house. To the left of us, a wild hedge created a border to our garden. To the right stood a small beech tree and about twenty metres in front stood a huge oak tree. I walked over to it.

"Hello, Dad."

This was another ritual of mine. Whenever I am at Oxon Hoath, I always go and visit my Dad under this tree, as there is something about it that reminds me of him. The tree is enormous. The branches spread out to create a large, natural dwelling around its vast trunk. I stepped under the branches into the welcome dim light created by the density of the foliage, and had the familiar warm feeling that I was stepping into Dad's house. I walked over to the trunk and stood facing it as I always did, taking in the details of the bark for a moment and remembering what Dad's eyes looked like; kind and direct, with a hint of amusement in them. The tree looked wise and loving, with its cracks and creases. I could hear Dad laughing.

"All right, Lizzie?" for some strange reason I have always been nicknamed Lizzie only within my family. "Been a bit bloody mad lately, hasn't it?"

I touched the rough bark as if I was touching his face and then leaned forward, closed my eyes and kissed it, taking a deep inhale through my nose. In that moment, I can always recall exactly how his cheek felt, warm and fleshy with a soapy, clean smell. I stepped back to look around the coveted area, snowdrops, crocuses, daffodils and bluebells grow under the tree in the spring and, at any time of year, it's a lovely spot to bring a cup of tea and sit and have a chat with Dad.

Bluebell time is my favourite as they remind me of him. He often sang a silly, repetitive song about bluebells being blue because they are blue that went on and on and on. He would usually sing it when we were trapped in confined spaces like the car and repeat it until we all chorused, "Dad!!!! Shut up!" For some reason it amused him and for us, it was one of those infuriating Dad things that we enjoyed.

There were no bluebells today; that time of year had passed. I sat down and leant against the strong bark and watched Leela play. This was one of her favourite spots, too, providing a cool shade for her to play in when the sun got too hot. Dad would have got tremendous joy out of watching Leela. I could just hear him laughing and commenting as she busily ran around hiding her ball, finding it again, doing a bit of digging, pouncing on a stick, running around the tree trunk a few times and then doing the same thing all over again. It was a playground in a world full of playgrounds for her.

"Hellooo!" I heard a familiar voice talking to Josh back at the van and made my way over. It was Marcy, the retreat co-ordinator and the slowest-talking, most relaxed New Yorker anyone could ever meet.

"Oh hi, Lianne," she drawled, gliding across the grass with her elegant watery walk. "It's lovely to see you, how's it going for you guys?"

Marcy had popped over to see if we had everything we needed. She had worked at the house since it opened as a retreat centre ten years before and Oxon Hoath just wouldn't be the same without her. I think everyone who visits grows as fond of Marcy as they do of the house. As well as giving a warm welcome to anyone who steps into the gates, she also adds a good dollop of eccentricity to the place. Her tall, willowy figure can appear anytime and in any place in the house and always when you least expect it, as she knows every nook, cranny and short cut. It's not unusual to leave Marcy tapping away at the keyboard in the office, walk the forty seconds it takes to get to the bar and find her standing behind it, grinning wildly and ready to serve you and offering no explanation as to how she got there. If asked, she would let out a guilty laugh and then look bewildered for a moment as if searching to remember how she got there herself. It was always good to see Marcy. She slowed your pace down considerably whether you wanted her to or not. She had been a great support to us since the beginning of our time at Oxon Hoath, always ready to promote a new idea or workshop.

Once Marcy had glided away, we put up the awning, which was to be our working space when Jack arrived, and made lunch. We were sitting in the sunshine munching on the remains of dahl and rice outside our office/home in a beautiful English country garden when Jack joined us.

"Well, you guys look pretty stressed, you need to get out of the office more!" Jack bellowed sarcastically, before roaring with laughter. Originally from New York and now living in London, the only thing medium-sized about Jack is his actual physical size. Everything else about him is larger than life; his personality, his heart, his voice, his opinions, his confidence and most of all, his infectious laugh, which is always readily available.

It's an injustice to even try and give Jack a title. Although his professional life started in the music industry and he is still a musician, he is also a great coach. Whether with leaders, performers or someone he just met at a bus stop, he wastes no time in using his skill of connecting and encouraging the best out of people. It's not a job, it's a way of life for Jack.

Jack had been dealing with the clients so far and he plunged straight in with their requests. They had asked for a treasure hunt, team-building and health management and he had said "yes, yes and yes" to each request. It was a relief to hear, because if they had asked for flying trapeze, pole dancing and sword swallowing, the answer would have been the same. The last time Jack said no was probably around 1968 and he probably changed his mind later on.

We spent the next few days working in this perfect environment, with Leela running around with us. The job finished on a high and we celebrated with dinner on the lawn on one of those rare balmy English summer evenings when the light is exceptional and the air is heavily scented with the sweet smell of jasmine, and filled with the sound of birds. Leela was still exploring the garden as if she had just discovered it, and I felt light and happy living our dream.

The dusk was making our eyes blur and we decided to call it a day. We strolled back to the van and rolled the door shut. Tonight was a massive step up from our comedy start not even a week ago. The air was warm, the sky clear, Leela smelt of summer meadows and we were in our little palace in a private piece of paradise, with no one to disturb us.

"Goodnight, sweet dreams," Josh said.

"Goodnight, sleep tight," I answered

"Woof." (You know who said that!)

Chapter Twenty-Eight

BUDDHAFIELD

The gentle call of a wood pigeon awoke us. I let Leela out of the van and she ran to play with her friends, Rubin the rabbit and Berty the badger. After making tea, we sat in bed and enjoyed the smell of sweet summer grass drifting into the van. The birds twittered with joy and the warm summer breeze danced on our skin as we stepped outside to do our yoga and set a positive intention for the day. A bluebird landed on my shoulder and sang a song of love as we sat and ate fresh strawberry jam spread on perfectly round wholemeal rolls, washed down with real coffee. Josh put on his Lederhosen and went to chop wood...

Okay, okay, it wasn't quite like that, but it wasn't far off, honest! We had a perfect start to the day, the sun was shining and we had plenty of muesli in.

It was time to move on again and we were heading to Buddhafield Festival in Somerset. Like most festivals, it was offering music, workshops, cafés, camping, unusual and interesting people from all walks of life, stalls and therapies. It also had a strictly 'no dogs' policy, so we dropped Leela off at a friend's house in Brighton before heading further west for four days of fun, frolics and madness.

We arrived at the site at 2am and, as the gates were not due to open until 11am the next day, we joined the other early arivals that were sleeping in the car park. We woke early the next morning to the hustle and bustle of people who were waking up and getting in the queue. There was a feeling of excitement in the air and, looking out of the window, it reminded me of a travelling circus. There was the usual mixed array of colourfully dressed adults and children. Some were on foot with their rucksacks on their backs, or pushing wheelbarrows full of their possessions. Others were in live-in vehicles, which ranged from horse boxes and double-decker buses, to top of the range camper vans; for many people, these were their permanent homes. Maybe it was the way we were feeling, but everybody looked happy. We had just a short wait before we were signalled forward through the gates to be welcomed by the friendly staff.

I love the moment of arrival at a festival. It feels like coming home. Home to what, I am not sure, but it stirs up something, a primal feeling. It's like stepping back in time to how we would have lived, in villages that looked more like camps, with the smell of wood smoke and cooking drifting through the air and people getting on with life, chatting to friends and setting up their wares at temporary stalls, whilst kids chase each other, making up games and getting filthy. For the next four days, this farmland would be transformed into a village for the simple pleasure of enjoying each other's company.

We drove around on the lookout for a pitch that looked like it should have our name on it. The traders and staff were already set up, their homes dressed with flowers, coloured cloths, Tibetan prayer flags, branches and statues. There were tipis and yurts, as well as tents and odd makeshift dwellings. It was heart-warming to see how much effort people put into creating beautiful spaces and how, with a little imagination, something quite ordinary can become breathtakingly beautiful.

We spotted a reasonably sized space and parked up, making sure the van was level. After parking up late many a night over the years and getting straight into bed, only to wake up and find myself squashed against the side of the van with Josh's nose flattened against my back, breathing heavily down my spine, or finding in the morning that I had far too much blood in my head, I had got decidedly neurotic about being on flat ground. After all, it's the simple things in life that make it a joy!

After extremely precise manoeuvring, we used the side door to check we were level lengthways, the test being, did it continue to roll on its own when paced at the half open mark? Then we used Leela's tennis ball to see if it rolled widthways; did it roll when placed in the centre of the van floor? Once all tests were passed, I announced that I was happy and ready to get on with being carefree and we proceeded to put up the awning and decorate our pitch with silk flowers, saris, fruit, veg and anything else we could find in the van that was remotely decorative.

When we were satisfied we had 'festivalised' our pitch enough, we put the kettle on and sat in our garden ready to check out the neighbours and look at the packed programme. Across from us was a family in an old VW camper. Two adults and three children, who I guessed were aged between seven and fourteen, finishing off a late breakfast that had been spooned out of an old black pot on top of the fire. I turned my attention to the neighbour on our left in order to stop the feeling of sadness that there were only the two of us sharing our little festival home. There I made eye contact with a girl sitting outside her transit van, she introduced herself as Samara, an art student from Devon. She had a bright, fresh face and long dreadlocks that reached the waistline of her tie-dyed, bright purple dress. After a quick hello, she walked off with a bold spring in her stride to meet up with some friends.

We had been sitting watching the world go by for about half an hour and were contemplating another cuppa before heading off to explore, when the flap of the horse box pitched to the right of us swung open and, instead of a horse's head, the unshaven face of our neighbour appeared squinting at us.

"Alright, guys?" asked a deep, gruff voice that sounded like it had been seasoned over the years by several thousand packs of cigarettes, late nights and bottles of whisky.

"Hi, how's it going?" Josh answered

"Yeah," he said, and then seemed to forget where he was. He spent a few moments scratching his matted hair and running his hand over his unshaven face.

"Having a good festival so far?" Josh continued, trying to help him with his whereabouts.

"My name's Rainbow." He sounded relieved to remember who he was.

As he reached for his biker's jacket and slung it over his big, bare, tattooed chest, I struggled to put the name to the face for a moment, but then all was made crystal clear as he belched loudly and threw open the bottom part of his door to come out and join us. He was wearing a leather mini skirt and rainbow tights. Phew! Now it made sense! As he blundered towards us, I tried to put a personality to the appearance. *A party animal*, I thought and it crossed my mind that we might be in for a different kind of Buddhafield this year. Images of sleepless nights, tossing and turning trying to block out the sound of hard rock thumping out of portable mega speakers that were hidden inside his horse box, flashed into my head. As we offered him tea, I wondered if I should casually mention the 1am curfew?

As it turned out, Rainbow had just come back from six months in India where he had helped to build an orphanage in return for food and digs. He had plans to raise money with his carpentry business and get back there as soon as possible, to help build up sustainable communities in the places where local trade was suffering. We also learned that he was teetotal and had been for ten years. After he'd finished his peppermint tea, he wandered off to listen to a talk in the Dharma Parlour.

"Never judge a book by its cover," I said to Josh and just as I finished my sentence, a naked man and woman walked past hand in hand. They smiled at us and we waved back.

"More tea, vicar?"

After our second cup, we went for a wander out of the live-in field and down the narrow lane that led to the stalls, cafés and workshop structures. The lane was narrow and the surface was covered by massive sheets of tarpaulin that served to protect our feet from the thick mud that had been created by the large amount of rain that had fallen lately. It had obviously been laid to prevent the predictable chaos that would be caused by over two thousand people to-ing and fro-ing from one field to the next through this only available route. It was already soft underfoot and felt like one of those moving floors you find in the hall of mirrors at a funfair. On either side, there were hand rails made out of branches. They would most certainly come in handy as the ground got bouncier and more unstable over the coming days.

The festival field was alive with people doing their thing; people practising Capoeira, bangra and belly-dance classes going on and others doing circus skills, juggling and swinging poi balls.

We wandered into the Lost Horizons Café which was also a sauna, and joined some friends. It seemed like a third of Brighton upped sticks every year and came to Buddhafield and it was lovely to see so many familiar faces and enjoy the sense of being in a dream world. People were dressed in all kinds of stuff, evening wear, fancy dress, no-wear, fairies and elves were painting the faces of passers-by. Kids were running around with dirty faces and mischief in their eyes. It was heaven. There is a wonderful sense of connectedness and community at a festival, something that is so much more accessible when we are out of our concrete boxes and closer to nature and each other.

We ate early in an Indian tent and watched a band on one of the open mike stages and then decided to snuggle up in bed. The sound of African djembe drums in the distance got stronger and louder. There was obviously a big drum jam going on around one of the fire pits. It sounded exciting and at the same time deeply relaxing, I was soon fast asleep. I woke up some time later and heard the sound of sweet accordion and flute in the distance. The smell of wood smoke drifted into the van and, with it, a sense that all was well settled my soul as I felt myself sinking deeper into the futon mattress.

The next day began with a trip to the 'thunder box' compost toilet and, as to be expected, there was a queue of uncomfortable-looking faces worn by people dressed in night wear and wellies. Most of us tried to smile good morning at the sleep-blurred faces before standing in line and silently praying that the queue would move quickly. Every now and again, there would be an uncomfortable shuffle from the person in front who was in need of a new posture to give them the bowel control needed to maintain their dignity. As seems to be the case with most festivals, there was a distinct lack of toilets, which can lead to a traumatic start to the day. Occasionally, you get someone who has obviously timed it right and *not* forgotten they don't have the usual luxury of strolling into their own bathroom at short notice and finding it pleasantly unoccupied. They join the queue in a cheery mood, ready for a chat and there's nothing you can do at that point but fix a strained grin on your face and make one-syllable sounds at intervals, to feign some interest. The painful silence in the queue of people around you tells you that although their main concern is getting through this moment, they are also slightly enjoying your obvious torture and thinking, *there, but for the grace of God, go I.*

It was my turn to go and I walked up to the toilet that had just been vacated and proudly mounted the steps, as if about to receive an award for my bowel control, I was tempted to turn around at the top and make a speech. I decided against it. I have heard that there is a fine line between love and hate, and I intuited that this was the very time and place where I might just experience the wisdom that lay behind those words!

Inside, the toilets had been decorated with poetry and flowers and, due to the amount of fresh air circulating through the open space at the top and bottom of the door, it was sheer luxury compared to the usual chemical toilets often provided at these events. When I came out to wash my hands, the queue had about fifteen people in it and tension was mounting.

"Ah, that's better!" I announced. As I skipped merrily past, beaming at the pinched faces, a few people let out an involuntary laugh.

I went back to the van and put the pained, goofy toilet face on as I rolled open the door. Josh was still in bed.

"How is it?" he asked.

I grunted and kept the tortured look on my face.

"Better go," he said, jumping out of bed and, trying not to give in to the urge to laugh, as there were more serious matters at hand now, I watched as he slipped past me and disappeared through the awning.

After a blissful yoga class and a workshop of euphoric singing, I met up with Josh in the chai tent, a lively tent run by a community of people who spend their summers travelling the festivals and their winters on their land in Spain. They were serving simple organic food, delicious cakes and, of course, great chai, a hot, spicy Indian tea. There was a busker playing guitar and singing for a meal. Her sweet and powerful voice filled the tent, complimenting the chilled atmosphere.

The day was getting warmer and we moved outside after we had eaten and extended lunch to several cups of chai and another hour lying in the sun. I missed Leela. She would have loved running around this place meeting all the people that had showed up just to see her! She'd have been off nicking food when I wasn't looking and soaking up the friendly atmosphere. I wondered what she was doing now and it became obvious that wherever she was, she would be doing just that, running around, meeting people, on the lookout for food and being happy! What else was there to do in her world?

When Josh went off to a talk, I wandered around the stalls, browsing through clothes, jewellery and arts and crafts people had made or brought back from their travels around the world. I watched a carpenter finish off a beautiful miniature rocking chair whilst his wife carved an intricate design across the lip of a table. Behind them was an enormous truck that they lived in with their two young children. The side of it was open, revealing the beautiful, wooden, handmade interior, stacked to the max with their few belongings. It was lovely to watch them working together. They seemed content with their lives and they both had a healthy, earthy beauty about them, the kind acquired from living close to nature.

Their children were next to them, making small tables and chairs out of clay. We had got to know them over the years of going to festivals and the thing that always struck me was their sense of happiness and peace. This idyllic scene was a usual part of their day and it was inspiring to know that they lived like this all year round. Their children didn't go to school and their parents didn't concern themselves with the national curriculum, an absurd system where someone else decides for the masses what is important for them to know. Their kids followed their own passions and interests and their family lived by their own rules, growing their own food and making a humble living from the crafts they made.

I suppose many people would see them as taking the hard route in choosing not to have the usual modern-day trappings. Yet I knew this family and many other families that had chosen this route, and one thing they all appeared to have in common was a sense of peace and satisfaction, an essence of life that is so often lost in our frantic modern world where most people are so busy striving for more, in order to have a sense of peace and security 'one day'.

Our system drives us from a very young age to live for the future; to not be satisfied with what we have or who we are, but to strive for more. What if we brought our children up to be happy with what is? To love life and all the abundance it offers? What if they were left with that birthright of knowing they were okay just as they were? I felt a longing to put my theories into practice with my own children... to have the chance to help create a new generation away from the relentless goals of consumerism and status.

Feeling a curious mixture of inspiration and sadness, I moved away to find a quiet place to sit. Watching that family had stirred up feelings that were unwanted and difficult. As I walked past the Radical Midwife tent, the board advertising talks on natural home birth and attachment parenting screamed out, taunting me. I felt empty and then angry that I had no reason to go in, like a child who hadn't been invited to the party. I peeped in the open flap of the door. It looked safe and cosy. There were several women inside of various ages, some pregnant, some with babes in arms. The kettle was on, and large cushions and sheepskins were scattered across the floor. There was an elderly-looking woman with a kind face and a large, motherly body. At that point, my anger gave way to despair and I longed to go and lie down with my head on her lap. I wanted her to stroke my head and tell me it was okay, that I was still good enough, right enough, woman enough. A baby started to cry and as the mother put him tenderly to her breast, I turned away and walked purposefully up the hill to the meditation tent where Josh and I had arranged to meet.

I was still aching with grief when we took off our shoes and slipped inside. There were four or five people sitting around the room in deep meditation. They looked so peaceful and easy in their bodies. I turned my mind towards settling my spirit and letting go of the knot in my heart and sat down, placing my attention on my surroundings. Rich materials in beautiful colours hung on the canvas walls and were draped across the ceiling. At the front was a huge shrine with a gold Buddha, flowers, candles, incense and other smaller statues of various deities. People sat still with their eyes closed and a couple of people were lying down, their meditation session having been extended into an afternoon nap.

I closed my eyes and focused on the sounds around me. I could hear the gentle rhythm of people breathing peacefully and the sounds of the festival in the distance. I took my attention out of the tent first of all. I could hear the sound of children playing, a mixture of music coming from various locations in the camp, the inevitable sound of hand drums, a flute in one direction, a fiddle in another... the gentle hum of voices, peppered with the odd shout or roar of laughter. I let the sounds soothe me into a state of relaxation and float further into the distance as I brought my focus into the tent. I let my mind rest on the peaceful, rhythmic sound of Josh's breathing close beside me for a while and then finally brought my focus to my own breathing, letting go of the outside world. All was well and peaceful, my body was relaxed and there was no need to put anything right.

I sat for a while longer enjoying the stillness and then, to finish I ran through all the things I was grateful for in my life. By the time I opened my eyes about thirty minutes later, I felt a deep sense of contentment again and a willingness to trust that, if I was meant to be a mother, somehow, in some form or other, it would happen.

We had dinner with a few friends that night and went to dance to a lively gypsy band who had the whole tent jigging and rocking until the curfew began at 1am. We went back to the van after listening to a young girl play beautiful Spanish guitar as we sipped hot chocolate by the fire. A perfect end to the day.

We spent the next morning wandering in and out of debates and talks on alternative life and hope for the future, sitting in cafés and enjoying time with friends. After lunch, we were looking forward to 'Ecstatic Dance with Jewels'. Oh yes, it certainly did what it said on the tin. No drink or drugs were necessary, just a willingness to let go of the usual social restrictions of looking cool, being fashionably aloof and avoiding doing anything that may make you look foolish or, horror of horrors, 'untrendy', that are often associated with dancing in public.

By the time we got there, the workshop was in the warm-up stage. *Lovely Day* by Bill Withers was blasting out of the speakers and there was a rising atmosphere of excitement. The sun was beating down and most of the sides of the tent had been taken up to allow air to circulate. It was still hot in there, but nobody seemed to notice or care. It was three o'clock in the afternoon and broad daylight, apart from the reddish glow the sunlight was creating on the red canvas ceiling. Most people were already in the kind of dance state you reach in a club at one o'clock in the morning after a few sherbets.

The party was in full swing and, for the next two hours, we would be guided by Jewels on a journey into dance whilst being accompanied by a range of different music genres. Anything from Madonna, to heavy tribal African, to devotional temple music, could be sent through the giant speakers, each track intended to tempt us into letting go of our inhibitions and diving into dance. I know this practise well and yet it never ceases to amaze me how such a simple and ancient activity can encourage virtually anybody to free themselves of their judgements and restrictions and experience a depth of freedom that no drug or alcohol-induced state could ever bring.

A heavy, slow African rhythm with a beautiful, eerie female voice layered over the top entered under the fade-out of the Scissor Sisters. The atmosphere changed and Jewels, an attractive, spicy woman with a soothing voice, encouraged us to close our eyes and let the movement come through us. I felt lulled into a familiar state that only dance can bring me. I could feel Josh at my side. We didn't go to many things like this together as ecstatic dance wasn't his usual scene.

"Breathe and feel your feet on the earth." The welcome instruction drifted over the music and I felt myself drop a stage deeper. I love dancing slowly with my eyes closed.

"Free your mind and let go." I felt the room slip away, along with any stray thoughts that were still wandering around my head, and I felt a complete willingness to step into dreamtime. I could feel the crowd around me and felt fully immersed in my own experience.

It was probably about half an hour later, when the music became more upbeat, that I opened my eyes again. Everything was slightly hazy and I felt as high as a kite. As the energy and pace continued to crank up, I looked around the tent and saw so many familiar faces that I shared my life with in various ways that my heart swelled with happiness and a sense of community. Josh appeared at my side in an obvious state of bliss. We were dripping with sweat and right in the middle of it all, laughing and dancing with not a care in the world. Many people were dancing outside in the sunshine. Some had stripped off completely and cooled themselves off by rolling in a patch of mud that had formed in the middle of the tent, caused by the humidity and the pounding of wild dancing feet. It was nuts and perfectly normal all at the same time.

By the end of the workshop, we were all in a state of smiley bliss and flopped onto the floor to ground ourselves again and let the gentle temple music lull us into that state of relaxation that only comes after physical exertion. I leaned against Josh and smiled. It was great to have a partner in life that I could experience so many

different things with. We sat still and quiet together with
our eyes closed, feeling the people around us drifting out
of the tent, hugging each other, some laughing or crying.
I felt Josh move and I opened my eyes and looked at him.
In a flash, he put a daft, cross-eyed look on his face. I
rolled my eyes back in my head and sounded a deep
"Ommmmmm" and we both burst out laughing.

"Come on, you silly sod, get your stilettos and
handbag and pull yourself together," Josh belted out in
a northern accent. We got up and went outside. We had
brought our towels with us so we could get into the
shower quickly afterwards. We knew that most people
would head there eventually and, as the shower was a
little unpredictable, to say the least, like the thunder box
toilets, it was best to leave nothing to chance.

There were two shower cubicles behind a hedge at the
far end of the field. Well, when I say 'cubicle', I mean a
rickety metal frame holding up four sides of waterproof
canvas, the fourth side being the door that hooks
precariously onto a nail at the top of one of the poles.
The shower is a hosepipe with a nozzle on the end.
Sometimes, the wood-burning stove provides a glorious
gush of hot water and at other times, it just spits out a
cold, pathetic drizzle in a tired manner. Not the most
sophisticated piece of equipment, but absolute heaven
when you strike it lucky. We set off hoping for the best
and got there to find the shower area completely empty.
Elvis, the guy running the showers, proudly announced
that the water was well and truly at its best. Fantastic!
We dived into a cubicle each.

There is something special about showering outside.
Being able to look up at the sky and see trees around you,

hear the birds and smell fresh air. I turned on the tap and felt the hot water roll over my head and down my body, imagining I was under a tropical waterfall on my very own desert island. The world slowed down even more as I took my time washing the sweat and fatigue out of my hair and off my body, leaving just the feeling of exhilaration that the dance workshop had created.

By the time I turned off the tap, I was renewed and refreshed. I stood for a while, eyes closed, breathing deeply, enjoying the welcome cold air on my skin. Then, with a huge grin on my face, I unhooked the shower curtain, stepped out of the cubicle and found myself standing starkers in front of a long queue of disgruntled-looking people, all clutching their towels and shivering in the cool late afternoon air! I froze for a second, completely jarred out of my bliss, my grin slowly melting into a gormless, fly-catching shape as I tried to work out how long I had been in there and what on earth all these people were doing on my desert island! After a few stunned moments, I grabbed the towel that I had hung on a nearby tree, bumbled a quick apology, something about the tap being stiff and scuttled back to the van with my clothes clutched under my arm.

There is always a funny adjustment period after a festival. After a few days of being in an idealistic environment, the so-called 'real world' seems extra harsh and, quite frankly, ridiculous. Having left Buddhafield on a high, we stopped for fuel at a nearby garage. The newspaper headlines leapt out at us: *Social services failed to recognise pervert!* I went inside and couldn't help noticing the photo of a voluptuous-looking woman on the front of a gossip magazine; she was wearing a school uniform and seductively licking an ice cream, the type of image so normal in our society, so normal and sold so casually next to the sweets our kids buy. Confusion and frustration reign under our conflicting messages and values. There is a Native American expression that says that when you point a finger at someone, there are three fingers pointing back at you. Maybe there should be mirrors under our headlines instead of the usual name, shame and blame story!

The cover of another gossip mag informed me that a certain previously adored celebrity had dared to go out with a spot on their chin! And another had shown a fat midriff! Isn't that the kind of behaviour children get punished and labelled a bully for? Wouldn't it be great if everybody just stopped buying this crap! If money rules and profit make the choices, surely we have more power than we realise in our purses.

I moved my gaze away, not wanting my mood to dip, but left the garage feeling slightly deflated and longing for a world with more love and kindness in it.

Chapter Twenty-Nine

FRESH HOPE

Watching the early morning sunrise on Brighton seafront was well worth waking up early for. It was the day after Buddhafield and a fresh, cool morning with the promise of a warm day to come, and we were in no hurry to get started. We had arrived late the night before to pick Leela up and, when we woke we realised that she had come on heat. She was quiet and unusually uninterested in the fact that we were right in front of the sea. She didn't even want to join Josh for a walk on the beach and just sat as close to me as she could, looking confused.

I massaged her belly to reassure her. "You're lucky," I whispered.

It was getting on for six months since I had last had a period. My trusted consultants, Jonathan and Sarah, were sure that my body was not going through the menopause, although they were both confused as to why I had stopped menstruating. I wanted to trust that they were right, but it was hard when it didn't make sense. I didn't want to go to the doctor's. I wanted to keep my dream alive and be understood and, I was afraid of being told I was being ridiculous, that wanting a baby at my age was pie in the sky, so I stayed away and decided to wait a while longer.

I sat silently, staring out to sea with Leela's soft head resting on my lap. Here she was, experiencing her first surge of fertility whilst I was praying mine hadn't ended. I hate the word 'barren' and it kept circling round my head, again and again. Barren, dry, empty. I gave in to self-pity and let the tears run down my face. This wasn't supposed to happen, I was supposed to be a mum by now. Being childless never figured in my vision of how my life would turn out. All my soul-searching and questing for good health had only amounted to a body that was betraying me. This was wrong. This wasn't my story. What had I been doing for the last ten years? Why on earth hadn't I got on with it when I was younger, instead of trusting I could wait until I felt ready? I was so convinced I would get pregnant straight away! What a fool I had been. How naive to think I could make it happen at will.

My self-pity eventually faded away and I just felt ridiculous. How could my dog coming on heat make me feel so low!

Leela being on heat meant she would be spotting blood for about two or three weeks and, as we were in such a tiny space, we decided to pop into the pet shop to see what the general advice was on keeping mess to a minimum.

What we didn't expect to find was a whole range of underwear for dogs on heat! After the initial reaction of "No way!" wore off, we considered other options, such as covering everything with old sheets, or making Leela stay on the floor or outside. But as we had no idea how much blood she would lose and, due to her vulnerable behaviour, we didn't want to change the norm of her sleeping at the end of the bed. So we swallowed our pride and bought her a pair of knickers and some pads for her to sleep in. The rest of the time, we would stay outside as much as we could, so she could maintain her dignity and be as naked as a dog should be!

Shopping trip done and a windy summer's evening on the horizon, we stopped outside our favourite Indian takeaway, which was a little place just underneath the flat in Norfolk Square. Josh jumped out to get the curry and I waited in the van with Leela. Five minutes later, he came out empty-handed with a big grin on his face.

"Where's the curry?" I queried

"They're going to deliver," he said, looking very pleased with himself.

"You're kidding! Where are they going to bring it to?

"The seafront by King Alfred's. We'll go for a dinner table with a sea view tonight"

It felt bizarre as we sat watching the sea, drinking wine and waiting for our dinner to be delivered to our dinner table in the van, and even more bizarre was the vision of Leela sitting next to Josh with her new knickers on, her tail poking out of the tailor-made hole, looking decidedly miffed!

"This is bonkers," I said, giggling and welcoming the fuzzy impact the wine was having on me. Josh shrugged and filled our glasses. The bottle was almost finished by the time the curry man appeared grinning at the window, and we had reached that heavenly, giggly state that only an empty stomach and wine can give you. After a wonderful meal at the best table in the house, watching the sun go down into the sea, we turned the restaurant into our bedroom and hiccoughed ourselves into bed. I was getting to like this living in a van lark!

Next morning, after a swim in the sea and breakfast on the beach, we drove fifty miles or so along the coast to West Wittering. We had been meaning to go to there for some time, having heard about the miles of sandy beaches and diverse landscapes and, as hot weather was predicted for the next few days, we wanted to make the most of it.

West Wittering was indeed beautiful and, after a quick scout around, we concluded that there would be no chance of getting away with sleeping in any of the car parks or on the roadsides without causing a stir in the local community. The day was heating up and we were keen to get settled and onto the beach, so we checked out the only two campsites in town. One was fully booked and the other had one available pitch left and the owner told us it was in the 'no children' area. We regretfully announced that we were indeed childless and got the last available space in town. Well, I guess our situation had its advantages, although I would have preferred not to feel the ironic pang of disappointment at our good fortune.

It was a lovely campsite; small, with simple facilities and beautiful flowers in the well-kept gardens. We drove through the family area, which was really a bog-standard lawn area close to the toilets, shower and launderette. The 'No Children Area' was small and pretty and located in a quiet place at the back of the site. There were about six plots on the area, surrounded by trees. Our plot was by far the prettiest and was situated at the end, giving us a private garden. It also had two small trees on it that happened to be set at exactly the right distance apart for our hammock.

"Looks like we've struck gold again!" Josh said, as we pulled out the awning.

It was such a lovely spot and we further enhanced it with our portable garden, before lying in the hammock in the shade of the trees. Then, content that we had marked our territory, the three of us went off for a walk. We went out the back way and found ourselves in the most beautiful golden wheat field, quite stunning in the bright afternoon light. We walked along the path set around the outside of the field and about halfway around, we must have startled a bird that was nesting about a metre from the edge, completely hidden by the long stems of wheat.

As it flew up in the air, Leela sprang into action and disappeared into the wheat at full pelt. She would be completely invisible for a few seconds and then suddenly appear, as she jumped up high for a quick peep, only to disappear and reappear in a completely different part of the field. Each time, we would get a glimpse of her, white grinning teeth, pink tongue hanging out of her open mouth, ears held up momentarily by the height of her jump. She would do it several times before propelling herself back on to the path beside us, bouncing as if to entice us back in there with her. We threw a stick back in and she would do the whole thing again.

It was fantastic to watch. She was so at ease with her light, strong body that jumped and dived effortlessly at her command. I could imagine how the warm wheat would feel on her body and how the sound of the rustling stalks would excite her even more.

As I watched Leela throwing herself into life with the sole purpose of enjoying being alive, I remembered that feeling of letting my soul fly with my body for nobody's pleasure but my own, and the sense of relief and peace that came with it. I had felt angry with my body lately and disappointed in myself for not being able to get pregnant. I had created a story that I was a failure. The memory of how good my body could feel if I let it, opened my heart to myself again and, for the first time in months, I felt huge gratitude for my body. I stood in silent reverence as the sun shone high above the wheat fields, warming my face and body, and I vowed not to break my friendship with myself again, no matter what was to happen in the future.

After dinner that evening, we managed to get Leela into the hammock, where she lay on her back in the middle of us completely content, happy with her body, at peace with life. Her energy was infectious and we lay there in silence, being gently held and swayed, watching the sky darken into a beautiful azure blue, peppered with stars. It was a very precious evening at the end of a poignant day.

The weather stayed hot in the days that followed, so we spent our days on the beach and our nights in the hammock. Every day, we would go down to the sea and dive through the waves with Leela. In the water, we could enjoy our bodies with the same lightness and buoyancy that she experienced. We spent hours running into the sea against the waves, feeling the force of the tide against our legs and then diving under incoming waves to experience being washed back to shore.

My energy was restored and my faith in life was well and truly back by the time my forty-fourth birthday dawned at the end of the week. I woke up that morning feeling happy and relaxed and decided to spend the day around the van, sunbathing and doing yoga, with the aim of relaxing even more.

"Happy birthday." Josh gave me a big cuddle and announced that he would make breakfast, lunch and dinner as a birthday present. Sounded good to me!

I accepted his gift graciously and went off to the shower. My visit to the toilet made my birthday very special indeed, as I discovered that my period had started! The knowledge that after six months, my body had decided to make a turnaround, took some moments to sink in. What did this mean?

"I'll get pregnant this month," I said to myself, in a stunned whisper. "No, stop!" I said just as firmly, pulling myself back to reality before I was off, dreaming of sweet-smelling, chubby flesh and warm cuddles.

I wasn't going back there again; the disappointment I'd experienced each month was too painful. I decided just to be grateful, and promised myself I would not read too much into this. Life was good and I had plenty to be thankful for and if a soul had chosen us, I would get pregnant regardless of how much plotting and scheming I did or didn't do.

Pep talk over, I went back to Josh and announced the good news.

"That's fantastic!" he exclaimed. "What a birthday present!"

He insisted that we shouldn't read anything into it, although I did see a thousand and one thoughts wander across his eyes. It was a difficult thing to discuss. We had been through so many disappointments, it was hard to know whether to get excited again or not. In the end, we both decided to just stay open and not do too much planning. Life was feeling pretty good, anyway; anything else right now would be a bonus.

We ended up staying at the campsite for a week. A glorious, romantic week of sun, sea, sand and other words beginning with s. Early morning practice, long walks in the countryside and afternoon naps. It felt like a proper family holiday having Leela with us. She joined in the programme wholeheartedly, springing into action when we did and snuggling up for a nap in the shade when the day got too hot.

I loved those afternoon naps. She would totter over and plonk herself in the middle of us and do one of her huge, contented sighs. The underneath of her paws smelt of summer, that fresh, grassy smell that accompanies the warmth of the sun. I would lie and watch her sleep for ages, studying her white nose with the tiny black spots that looked like freckles. The longer black hair on her ears and back had been bleached a reddish-brown colour by the sun and salt water. Life had changed dramatically since she had tumbled out of that back door. She had brought a flow of magic into our lives that we could have never have envisioned. The fear of the unknown and the need to control had been replaced by a depth of trust I had always wished for.

As I drifted off to sleep, I could hear the steady rhythm of Josh's breath and the warmth of his body relaxing against mine. I felt like I was falling in love all over again.

Chapter Thirty

ONE WORLD CAMP

It was a bright, sunny Tuesday when we arrived at One World Camp to meet Sally and spend a few days camping together before the gig on the Saturday night. We had also taken advantage of our status as members of the band and had gained permission to have Leela with us.

The camp was held in a boarding school so the facilities were much more up-market than Buddhafield. As well as the usual marquees, yurts and tipis in the grounds, there was also a large sports hall, dance and yoga studios and the added bonus of an indoor swimming pool. Meals were to be served in a communal dinning area.

We made our way to the corner of a big playing field. Many people were staying in the indoor accommodation so there was lots of room in the camping area. Most of the band would arrive at the weekend and we wanted to save a big enough space so we could create a camp together. As we set up our pitch, Leela ran around, overcome with excitement at the amount of people there, all for the sole purpose of throwing her ball and making a fuss of her. It was going to be interesting setting boundaries for her here. She would be part of a much bigger pack once the rest of the band arrived.

The main feature of the festival was the workshops and the timetable was packed out from morning until night. There was something for everyone – a variety of subjects ranging from healing, yoga and soul retrieval, to cookery classes and political debates. I had already decided I was going to keep a firm hold of my work-shopaholic tendencies and only attend a chosen few!

Sally arrived soon after we did. The rest of the band would trickle in over the week. Once we were set up, we sat down for the official cup of tea and poured over the timetable for the week.

"Ooh, Mantric Tantric!" Sally said. "Sounds worth a go."

"I definitely want to go to Animal Healing with Leela," I said

"Find Your Inner Clown? That's a must, sounds completely bonkers. Ooh and Gong Healing!" Sally's adventurous nature was beginning to stir and she had an infectious way of taking mine with her. It was going to be an interesting week!

After much indecision, Sally and I decided to do Pranayama, starting at 6.30 in the morning, chanting in the yurt in the afternoon and Mantric Tantric in the evening. The rest of the day we would play by ear.

Next morning, true to my addiction, I left Leela tucked up in bed with Josh and met Sally outside her tent. Then, squinting in the morning sun with blankets tucked under our arms, we staggered off to the first session of the week.

The workshop was well worth getting up for. The session was well led by a gentle Indian woman and after an hour of *Pranayama –the science of breath*, we had deeply cleansed our lungs, balanced our male/female energies with nostril breathing, created bone massage of the face through sound and meditated. Highly recommended as a start to the day. We felt fantastic.

"That was well worth crawling out of a warm sleeping bag for," Sally said, as we sprang self-righteously past all the closed tents back to our camp, having done our morning practice, showered and had breakfast before most of the camp had even rolled over and grunted.

I spent the rest of the morning outside the van with Leela whilst Josh went for a swim. She was doing well at understanding the boundaries, considering we were in a big field with lots of other tents and vans. Every now and again, curiosity got the better of her and I would catch sight of her waggling rear end poking out of somebody's tent, probably looking for a morsel of food or a random cuddle. With a high recommendation from me, Sally went off to Laughter Yoga.

My friend Julie had once taken me to a Laughter Yoga class in Brighton. I had been one hundred percent opposed when she first mentioned it, as the idea of forcing myself to laugh seemed like a sad thing to do and it was only Julie's insistence that my opposition to it meant it would be good for me, that made me agree to give it a go. I did have one condition, though – that I could feign an asthma attack and leave if I wasn't convinced after twenty minutes!

The whole class consisted of various exercises involving forced laughter. The teacher, a genuinely happy-looking, rosy-cheeked woman, explained that if we pretended to laugh, eventually our natural endorphins would join in and we would find ourselves in the throes of authentic side-splitting hysteria.

We began with some warm-ups which involved stretching a little and allowing ourselves to smile, followed by letting a smile start in our toes and travel up our bodies, becoming a giggle around out midriffs and building into light laughter by the time it reached our heads. I felt irritated and self-conscious at this point but, seeing as we were only five minutes into the class, I gritted my teeth and continued to do as I was told. I pretended to pour myself a cup of giggles, threw it down my throat and then forced myself to chuckle loudly.

I had an intense dislike of everyone in the room by then and desperately wanted to go home. We were then instructed to point at somebody in the room and pretend they were the funniest thing ever. I lamely pointed across the room and mustered up a fake guffaw and the person I pointed at, pointed back with gusto and roared with laughter. Despite my resistance, I found it funny and a genuine laugh slipped out. I pulled myself together quickly, only to be taken over again by a ripple of pleasure as I sent my fake joy back in retaliation to her delight. About fifteen minutes in, I was taken over by true belly-clutching hysteria and I spent the next forty-five minutes laughing, chuckling, giggling, roaring, guffawing and snorting myself into a state of ecstasy. It was brilliant! I sailed out of the studio feeling that I would never take anything seriously again.

As there was no sign of Sally or Josh by lunchtime, I set out to go to lunch on my own. There was a mixture of people in the dining room. Like all festivals, the ages ranged from nought to ninety-plus. Most people looked better groomed and cleaner than the Buddhafield crowd, but were just as vibrant and healthy, wearing colourful clothes and easy smiles. I picked up my meal, which was a concoction of soya meat stew, salad, sauerkraut, vegetables, corn bread, and a pudding of stewed fruit.

I sat down on one of the many communal tables next to a friendly-looking man wearing a colourful robe. He had sparkly eyes and a peaceful, 'wise monk' look about him. He smiled at me as I sat next to him and I felt in good company.

I arranged my dinner, put my tray on the floor and picked up my fork, ready to tuck in. At that point, Monk Man turned to me and said, "If you feel uncomfortable sitting next to me, it's okay, just let me know."

"Eh?" I articulated, a fork full of sauerkraut hovering at my lips

"I am a healer, I pull to the left. I'm always in healing mode so you may find me drawing negative energies out of you. You're sitting on my left, you see. Some people find that uncomfortable."

I lifted my lips upwards in a token smile of 'okay' and stuffed my food into my mouth.

Never judge a book by its cover, I thought yet again.

"I spread light wherever I go, I can't help it, it gets me in trouble sometimes."

I stared open-mouthed and said nothing. Mr Monk stared deeply into my eyes. I broke his gaze and swallowed another forkful, along with a more unsavoury word describing my thoughts about him.

"I get visits, from the twins, they guide me."

I started to feel like my space was being invaded.

"The twins are light years away. We communicate through the twelfth star," he continued. Mr Monk obviously had a good filter system that enabled him to just talk at people.

Now, I actually don't have any problem with believing that all this is possible, but I do get suspicious of people when they have a need to tell you these things ten seconds after you meet them. I also felt slightly suspicious of the fact that although Mr Monk had the sensitivity to pick up vibes from beings light years away, he still had difficulty detecting the lack of interest beaming out from the person sitting less than a metre from him. I spent the rest of my lunch improving my ability to swallow corn bread whole in order to make a quick exit.

"I sense you feel uncomfortable now." Mr Monk finally picked up the vibe as I stood up hastily to get away and knocked over my cup.

"I guess people find it hard to stay around you for too long. Amazing, isn't it?"' I smiled warmly at him and ran.

"How was it?" I said to the back of Sally's head, as I walked outside and found myself straight behind her.

She turned around and her irritated face said it all. "I laughed more when I had my car nicked," she muttered through tight lips

"Sorry," I mumbled pathetically. There is only one thing worse than choosing the wrong workshop to go to, and that is choosing one for someone else who skips off enthusiastically with great expectations and hates it. Fortunately, we spent the next half hour creased up with laughter at how unfunny she'd found it. By the time we had finished, she had tears streaming down her face so I guess it did the trick after all.

"Still fancy Mantric Tantric tonight?" asked Sally.
"Okay, I'll give it a go."

Mantric Tantric was held in a cosy, candle-lit room
inside the school. The facilitator was a warm American
guy with a hint of Deep South in his accent, who
informed us that we would be taken on a journey
through the chakras. Chakras are data banks of spinning
energy located at the pubic bone, below and above
the naval, the heart, throat, brow point and crown,
each one relating to different parts of us emotionally,
spiritually and physically. The session would focus
on each one in turn, giving us a chance to heal and
cleanse anything we were ready to let go of. Sounded
good so far.

It began with a relaxing meditation and then, as a
drumbeat slowly began to get louder and more intense,
we were encouraged to make sounds, dance and thrust
ourselves into our base chakras. I thrust away, yelling an
"Uh" sound, pounding my feet rhythmically on the
floor, with the facilitator's Deep South twang cheerleading
me on, as if he wanted to drown out the thoughts that I
was being drafted in to some weird evangelical cult. I
carried on pounding and shouting and shaking my head,
at the same time moving away from Sally, because I
knew that if I caught her eye, we would end up giggling
like naughty schoolgirls.

I was kind of enjoying myself, but was also acutely
aware of the cynic roaming around in my head. She had
her nightdress on but was still showing signs of insomnia.
I closed my eyes tightly and had a little chat about giving
things a chance, before putting a cup of cocoa in her
hand telling her to bog off to sleep.

I carried on thrusting and 'uhhhing' and progressed to jolting and breathing heavily. It took a while, but I eventually let go of the suspicion that this was payback time for Laughter Yoga and Sally had actually slipped out of the workshop and was smirking to herself over a beer in the bar, and allowed myself the chance to experience it.

The first three chakras are quite physical as they relate to the more earthy business of being in the body. By the time we had chanted and moved through those, I felt as though I was fully inhabiting my body. Our 'minister' was a great guide and kept us focused. We slowed down as we journeyed into the upper chakras and eventually ended up on the floor in a meditation, before we lay down to complete the session in silence. I felt tingly and calm.

I took my time to gather my things and myself together and wander outside. Sally was outside, looking as content as I felt. We went back to camp with the bare minimum of words passing between us.

"Brilliant."

"Lovely."

"I feel so good."

"Me too."

"See you in the morning."

"Goodnight."

Chapter Thirty-One

THE GIG

Paul, our bandleader, arrived on the morning of the gig with his three kids and a new band member I had never met before, who he introduced as Gabriel. Paul has a way of turning everything into a party. He is loud, coarse, full of love and instantly likeable, the kind of person that walks into a pub full of strangers and comes out having invited everyone to Christmas dinner.

"All right, champions?" Paul burst into our day with his usual air of chaos, hands full of bags, car full of instruments, yelling and hugging everyone in turn as if they were the long-lost love of his life.

Within minutes, everyone had met Gabriel and been given a brief history of each other's lives, along with a description of our talents and how brilliant we all were. Then he was off in a whirlwind of activity, putting up his tent, organising the kids, making pasta, interspersed with cups of tea, custard creams and funny stories of what he had been up to, and plans for the gig.

It was great fun having him and his family around. His kids spent the rest of the day entertaining themselves with poi balls, juggling, badminton and football, had several arguments, made up again, and generally made themselves at home. The circus was in town and there was a festive spirit in the air.

Leela joined in with the kids as if she was one of them. She was like a magnet for children and seemed to adapt her behaviour to suit their age. Yesterday, I had watched as she made up a game with two toddlers, gently pouncing on the ground rather than on their hands as they went to pick up the ball, and running around in a comical circle to avoid jumping up at them when she got over-excited, which was normally something she couldn't help herself from doing. The toddlers had giggled and squealed with delight at their furry playmate. It was ironic that I had a dog that had such a way with children. Today, I watched again as Leela adapted her style to fit in with Paul's kids, who ranged between eight and fourteen, and was soon bossing them about, nicking their stuff and making them laugh just in time, before she got sent away.

The day got livelier and louder as more and more band members arrived for the gig. I had missed seeing everyone at rehearsals over the last few months. It is a lively band reflecting the type of music we play, called Maracatu, and the Brazilian spirit of its roots. We had a rehearsal in the middle of our camping circle to prepare us for the evening and 11pm found us all backstage in the school corridor, strapping our instruments on and getting ready to perform.

Everything about Maracatu is exciting. The instruments are beautiful. The large bass drums, known as alfias, are made of wood, rope and skins, and are played with wooden sticks, as are the snares. The shekeres are made of a net of beads loosely tied over the dried skin of a plant that belongs to the pumpkin family, giving it a lovely, round, womb-like shape and a wonderful sound. There are also the cow bells and congas, although tonight we had substituted timbas for congas as they are a much lighter instrument and easier to carry.

I love that moment before you go on stage and it is so much more intense when there are lots of you, all feeling the same tingle of anticipation. There was a mounting sense of excitement in the dark corridor, people searching for water and earplugs, checking their instruments were strapped on securely. The dancers were adjusting their traditional white dresses and headbands and running through the choreography just one more time.

We got the two-minute warning and lined up in order. Paul's presence became even more noticeable and central to everything. All eyes were on him and there was a moment of hush. He raised his hand and signalled for the bells and shekeres to start, counted us in – "Four, three, two, one" – and the corridor was filled with Brazilian magic, teasing the crowd into a cheer. Paul signalled for the snares to start and then myself and Alex on the timbas. The crowd cranked up with each layer and a big roar came from them as the alfias' booming sound cut through the other rhythms and thudded into everyone's hearts.

We were off, parading through the cheering crowd and onto the stage and the crowd was up and dancing already. Paul was at his biggest and best, having fallen in love with everyone in the band, the crowd and the world. This was him in his element and he had an infectious way of bringing out 'the vibe' in everyone. I looked around at the band; everyone looked elated and going full throttle.

Alex was grinning wildly next to me. We had played a lot together in the past and I was glad he was here on what was possibly my last gig with this band. Josh was giving it some welly on the shekere. He wasn't actually a band member but, true to his party style, Paul had insisted he joined us for at least one number, so there he was, big, colourful shirt on, huge grin on his face, proudly throwing his chekere from side to side!

The dancers joined us as we started the second number and raised the level of excitement again, bringing in that hazy sensation of being in a dream and feeling fully alive at the same time. The power of the rhythm of Maracatu easily takes you into a trance-like state and it is nigh on impossible to keep your feet still.

The gig lasted about an hour and by the time we finished, we were all dripping with sweat and totally ecstatic. The crowd went crazy and brought us back twice for an encore, until Paul eventually wrapped the whole evening up in his charming style.

"Thanks for being a great crowd. We're all bleedin' knackered and off to get pissed, see you in the bar," and we obediently followed our orders from the Maestro.

Chapter Thirty-Two

MY FAMILY AND THE OTHER
ANIMALS

It was my younger sister Maxine's fortieth birthday party, and, as we were driving up to Manchester after leaving One World Camp, we prophesised about the big bash. I find watching my family hugely entertaining and, over the years, Josh has taken to the sport as well. We have agreed that the fundamental difference between a visit to our respective families is that when you go to his, you are entertained by the hosts, and when you go to mine, the hosts *are* the entertainment.

Maxine, who avoids any kind of stress, had stated very clearly that for her fortieth, she wanted to go away somewhere close by for a few days with her husband Rick, as that way she could enjoy a bit of down time but not be too far from the kids. When they got back, she wanted to have a quiet family barbeque. Rick, who is madly in love with his wife and loves to indulge her suggested they go to Majorca for two weeks, but Maxine explained that it was too far from the kids. So then, he came up with the idea of a week in the Maldives instead, for which she politely thanked him and pointed out that the Maldives is slightly further than Majorca and a week was still too long. After presenting her with the idea of going to Las Vegas for a weekend, she bluntly told him that if he had learned anything at all about her in the twenty-six years they had been together, then he would know that she would rather bang nails into her own forehead than go to Las Vegas and, would he please take her to see a show in London and book them overnight in a nice hotel.

That did it. Rick finally picked up on the subtleties, got them tickets to see *Wicked* and booked them into a hotel in London. Then his generous nature got the better of him and he invited about fifty people over for a party the day after they got back. Well, he nearly got it right!

"It'll be chaos and changes of plans all day," said Josh

"I know," I said. "It'll work out, though. It always does somehow."

"That's because Kaye will do it," Josh said. "She'll say she won't, but she will and Maxine will say she will, but she won't."

He had them to a tee. My sisters react in completely opposite ways to stress. Kaye runs around refusing to do anything at all, whilst doing everything and insisting she feels perfectly chilled out. Maxine, on the other hand, says she will do everything but freezes, blanks everything out of her mind and goes and does her hair and puts her make-up on. It's not uncommon for Maxine to invite everyone for Sunday roast and then phone up about 3pm to see if anyone has a spare roast chicken they could bring, as she doesn't seem to have one in.

"Kaye will run round like a headless chicken all day, change the menu seven times and then do a chilli," I laughed. "Maxine will put the oven on and then go and get in the bath. Paul will end up doing the barbeque and Rick will refuse to help until the last minute and then burst into action."

"And what about you, what's your role?" This was his way of letting me know I was just as much 'the sport' for him as everyone else was.

"You'll stand in the middle of it all, practising your party moves with the dogs and not even pretending to be of any help," he added.

No point in arguing with that one. Josh had an uncanny way of predicting the future...

Kaye called first thing in the morning in full family party mode.

"I've decided I'm not getting too involved today. Rick planned this so he can do most of it. I'll do a salad and make a cheesecake, but that's it. I'm not doing anything after that. I'll just tidy round and do a bit of gardening, and I might sort the garage out. I've got vegetarian sausages in the fridge; I could do a hot pot for the vegetarians. No, leave it, we'll get pizzas in, nobody's expecting that much and even if they are, it's not my party. I'll ring Maxine and give her a shopping list. At least she can have a few bits in if people are hungry later. No, I'll ring Rick. He organised all this, he should do the shopping."

When we turned up at Kaye's an hour later, she was making a chilli and clearing out the airing cupboard.

Leela burst into the house and Marley, Sam and Cookie ran to meet her. Everything stopped so we could watch the dogs perform their welcome dance, catch up on the gossip and establish the hierarchy.

"I've made a veggie one and a meat one," said Kaye, drawing our attention to the huge pots on the stove. "That's it now, I'm relaxing." With that, she walked into the airing cupboard and got out the ironing board.

I resisted an urge to practice a dance move as Josh wandered out of the back door looking for my brother-in-law, Paul. Paul was hiding in the garage at the bottom of the garden, knowing that at some point he would be called on to sort out an 'emergency' at Maxine's, like rigging up a music system or making sense of the instructions for some garden lights. Not that Paul shies away from do-it-yourself. In fact, he does everything himself. In the past, he has designed and built the extension on the house, landscaped the garden, built his own computers and designed and turned part of the garage into a gym, as well as creating remote controlled lighting and music in the living room. You name it, he will turn his hand to it.

Mid afternoon, Kaye and I called round at Maxine's to see how things were. Sure enough, she was upstairs with a towel round her wet hair, trying on a few outfits. The kitchen looked like an IKEA showroom. It had obviously been scrubbed clean that morning and then the bath got run. Rick was pretending the party had nothing to do with him and was refusing to put up the marquee they had borrowed, although rain clouds were threatening to turn the garden party into a disaster. Not that he is a stranger to do it yourself either, it's just that somehow his skills of building his own garage, putting a loft conversion in, landscaping the garden and running his own business don't seem to emerge when there is something simple to do, like putting up a Christmas tree on time or, putting a plug on a household appliance, or, and, more pressingly in that moment, putting up the frame of a marquee!

Guests were due to arrive from 7pm onwards and it was about 6pm when everyone suddenly sprang into action, organised by Kaye. Miraculously, all the salads, quiches, sausage rolls, crusty bread, rice and chilli appeared on the table, the marquee was pieced together by Paul, after Josh had made several botched attempts out of the materials provided, Rick jumped up and set up a fantastic bar on the tressel table by the patio doors, my dance moves were perfected and Maxine came downstairs stunningly dressed, with her three immaculate daughters behind her. It was party time! Once again, we had effortlessly achieved our goals and felt we had every right to let our hair down and have a great night.

By 8.30, things were cranking up. The buffet was announced 'open', and I noticed Josh had settled himself down next to the food table with a beer, fully intent on enjoying the scene that was about to unfold before him. He caught my eye and laughed guiltily. Feeding time at any of our family occasions has always been a source of amusement for Josh. He likened it to the Red Cross arriving in a war zone after months without any general supplies. I stood at the other side of the table and struggled to find any words to defend my beloved family from such a heartless description.

The tin foil was off and within seconds, people were fighting for their lives – oodles of chilli mounting up on plates, crisps being shoved down throats in between hastily lashing copious amounts of butter on door-wedge-size slices of bread. Wives elbowing their nearest and dearest out of the way so they could grab a piece of cheesecake, mothers hastily throwing a sandwich together and hurling it in the direction of their offspring in the hope it would keep them occupied for at least another ten minutes whilst they filled their boots.

There was only one way to cope and that was to fend for yourself. After I had filled my own belly, I thought I'd be gracious and take some food out for Mum. She was sitting in the garden with her partner, Joe and sister, Auntie Maureen.

Mum and Maureen were applauding and whooping and shrieking loudly as an impromptu dance performance by the kids, spontaneously choreographed by the eldest niece, Lauren, came to an end. Joe, who fortunately is well armed with tons of patience, was hastily moving their wine glasses out of the way to prevent them being knocked over, as their alcohol-fuelled enthusiasm made them oblivious to their surroundings; a job that would get increasingly more difficult as the night progressed.

I put the plates down and watched the next number, which was actually a repeat of the first, being performed again due to public demand. Mum and Maureen were chatting behind me.

"I think dancing's a great way to keep fit," said Auntie Mo, a great dancer herself who went regularly to the local line dancing class.

"Oh yes," Mum said, "that and diet, Maureen. You can't get by on a few chips a day, you know. You should eat better. No matter what, I get my nutrients. I have a tin of fresh fruit salad every day!"

I chuckled all the way back to the kitchen to get them another bottle of wine. *Must write that one down*, I thought. *Classic!* As I put the fresh bottle of wine down on the table in front of them a few minutes later, I heard a snippet of their new conversation.

"Our Lianne said that they don't really celebrate Christmas in Israel," Mum said,

"Don't they?" Maureen looked confused

"No, they're Jewish!" Mum said authoritatively.

"Oh, aren't they a miserable lot!" With that cultural observation, Maureen stood up to do the Macerena with her granddaughters.

Back in the kitchen-diner, a circle had formed and everyone was fully immersed in there own version of Pink's *Cuz I Can* as it blasted into the room. I joined in wholeheartedly. I looked at my sisters, eyes closed, each with glass in hand, having completely let go of any signs of stress that the party would flop. In fact, even if it did flop now, they would just remain blissfully unaware and still dance and sing their hearts out until the early hours!

All of Rick's family had now arrived – his two brothers and three sisters and their partners and, being Irish they added a good blast of high spirits to the evening. Rick was on form and doing his Elvis impressions and comedy party dances. Paul was rewiring an old speaker so we could crank it up even more. '*Paradise by the dashboard light*' came on and Max and Rick were about to do their party piece of miming the whole thing to each other, I plonked myself down on the settee to take it all in. All five of my sister's children were in the room, giggling and laughing together. I thought of all the family parties we had had as they were growing up, the different stages of their lives I had witnessed, from being swung around by their mums and dancing on their dads' backs, to today, partying alongside their parents, all good friends, lives shared and intertwined.

I loved being a part of it, but I longed for my own family, too. What was it like to party with your child? To watch them grow and change? To sit and giggle together in the morning as the previous night was recalled? A sudden sadness came over me and I slipped out of the house and into our van that was parked in the driveway. I had had too much wine. It was time to stop thinking, stop feeling and go to sleep. I used to get into such a state each month when my periods were regular and then not having any had stopped me being so obsessive about what my body was doing and where I was on my cycle. I didn't want to start counting days again now I had had a period, being on that awful rollercoaster of hope, joy disappointment and sadness. I wanted to just live life day by day and see what it had to offer me.

Chapter Thirty-Three

WALES

Wales was our next port of call as we wanted to explore the possibilities of living there. The vast open spaces and natural beauty appealed to us although, both being sun-worshippers, we had reservations about the weather. As we drove over the hills of North Wales, we spotted a lake that was picture-postcard perfect. The beauty of the land coaxed us down a number of tiny roads until one bumpy track led us right to the edge of the lake.

It was a beautiful evening; the water was completely still, proudly reflecting the mountains and the lush green vegetation surrounding it. We stood quietly and soaked in the awesome stillness, before Leela bombed up and dropped a stone in front of us. I picked it up and threw it high into the air. It landed a few feet in front of us and the picture was broken as perfect circles rippled out from the centre. We watched mesmerised as the water became still once again, reflecting a crystal-clear image of the solid mountains delving deep below the surface of the lake. It was an obvious place to set up camp for a while and once we had done that, we spent the rest of the evening walking around the lake until the rain drove us indoors for the night.

It felt very romantic in the pitch black and we felt really grateful for all the times we had struck lucky with our places to sleep. The more we seemed to trust and expect that things were going to work out, the easier things were happening for us and we both had a strong sense that life was moving in the right direction. Every day we had been on the road, we had done a meditation together, asking for guidance and clear signs that we were on track. Little gifts like our lakeside paradise were signs to us that we were.

During our stay in Wales, wherever we went, we were bathed in natural beauty. It was a real retreat and we spent most of it in silence. Each day, the three of us walked for miles, mostly in the rain but with some glorious moments when the sun burned through and showed this Promised Land in all its splendour. We found waterfalls and forests, lakes and amazing views on beautiful hilltops. It was a precious time to meditate and dream.

A week of wandering led us to Shell Island, miles and miles of sand dunes and a beautiful beach. It was windy and wet, but it felt comforting to be by the sea and amongst the sand dunes. Leela dived into the new scenery, ever ready to explore and enjoy herself to the max. She loved windy weather. It was as if everything moved just for her. The sand whipped up her nose, teasing her to pounce into the dunes and dig. Leaves, shells and sticks taunted her to chase them whilst her ears flapped around her face. Playing peek-a-boo with the world, her aliveness and passion for life never dwindled.

I, on the other hand, had taken a U-turn. I just didn't understand it; it had happened literally overnight. I went to bed feeling ecstatic and so in love with life one night and woke up the next morning feeling lost and tearful. I was trying my best to keep a smile on my face whilst grumbling inside about the weather. The wind was annoying me, I was tired of getting sand in my eyes, I was fed up with the damp and the dull chill it created. We hadn't been able to dry anything properly over the last few weeks, which meant all my socks were damp and my feet hadn't been dry for days.

The other thing that I couldn't quite shake off was the smell of upholstery in the van, that seemed to be becoming more prominent. It was just a general new car kind of smell. I had noticed it when we first got the van and we had burned oils and incense in it as part of the process of putting our stamp on it. It seemed to go after while, or at least I had stooped noticing it. Now, it was back with full force and it irritated me every time I stepped into the van.

We had had one season since last October, wet and warmish with a damp chill in the air and, although I was loath to admit it, I felt angry about it. I once read that you can tell a lot about a person by how they react to the weather, and that observation was adding to my irritation! Only the day before, we had gone for a long walk on the beach. It had been blowy and wet and exhilarating to be out in the mass of open space, with just dunes, beach, sea and Leela. I had enjoyed the feel of rain on my face and the smell of sea salt and it felt great to sit around the fire in the evening, feeling salty and gritty and ruffled by the wind. Yet now, here

I was less than twenty-four hours later, equating all the same circumstances to utter misery. Maybe I was coming down with a cold, I thought. We had spent so much time in damp clothes, it would hardly be surprising. I decided to keep how I was feeling to myself, in the hope that it would blow over as quickly as it had descended.

After a couple of days, we headed back inland with the intention of checking out South Wales. We drove all afternoon and evening, slowed down by the driving rain. It was pitch black when we pulled into what we presumed was a car park and cuddled up in bed. I hoped I would be in better spirits by the morning. The smell in the van had got so far into my nostrils, I could taste it with every meal and the thick, grey blanket of cloud we had driven under all day was making me feel claustrophobic and panicky.

The morning light revealed that we had stumbled on yet another magical place. Reminiscent of a scene from *The Mists of Avalon*, a cold mist rolled eerily across a beautiful lake surrounded by trees and bushes of the deepest, darkest green, the air smelt strongly of musty, damp wood and fresh leaves and there was a hush of anticipation in the wet, hazy aura that surrounded everything. It felt like a land where no one else had ever been. I was half expecting to see a rowing boat move eerily out of the grey mist, skilfully guided by a figure in a hooded coat. My dark mood lifted as we stood entranced, watching the mist roll away to reveal the reflection of the trees and sky above the lake.

I was revived and ready to embrace life again as we walked back to the van, but as soon as the door rolled open, the smell hit me again. I looked out of the window and felt the clouds pushing down on me. I looked over at

Josh. He was clearly enjoying himself and I didn't want to burst his bubble with my sledgehammer of a mood, so I carefully suggested that we found an internet café and checked out the weather in the rest of Wales.

"Maybe we could head for a sunny spot and have a chance to dry out a bit," I suggested. I was doing my best to make it sound like a sensible passing thought and Josh, in his happy-go-lucky state, thought it was a good idea.

We drove most of the morning and eventually came to a small village with an internet café. Josh sat outside with Leela and a hot drink and I went in to see where the weather would guide us to next. I clicked on the five day forecast and a map of the British Isles came up for each day. It didn't look good. Rain, rain and more rain; my heart sank. This was unbearable, we still hadn't started the procedure of getting Leela a passport which apparently would take six months, and it was looking like the great British summer had peaked a few weeks back and was on track to slide into a wet Autumn. Then I saw a sun sign on Saturday. It was in the South East, so I clicked on the report and it informed me that Saturday was going to be hot around the Brighton area. It was Thursday now and if we headed back today, we could find a campsite and enjoy at least one blissful day of sunshine.

I went out and suggested it to Josh and thankfully he agreed. The thought of blue skies, warm air and staying dry for a few days obviously appealed to him as much as it did to me. Although I was mega keen to get out of Wales and down to the South East as soon as possible, I smiled and agreed to take our time when Josh suggested we meander back along the scenic route. We drove all day, with a few welcome breaks to stretch our legs and let Leela burn off some energy and eventually pulled into a lay-by about 11pm.

In the morning, I woke to the smell of damp uphol-stery and the sight of heavy grey cloud and, in my overwhelming desire to get as far away from Wales as possible, I blurted out that I wasn't interested in the view at all and wanted to get on the motorway as soon as possible, because if I didn't get to see blue skies soon, I would suffocate, wither and die!

I think Josh was slightly surprised by my outburst, but the strength of it gave him the wisdom not to question me and we drove to the South East as fast as we could. Rick, our ex-neighbour, phoned as we were bombing along the M4 to tell us we had a ton of post, so we figured we should head there and spend the night on the seafront.

By the time we got to Brighton, it was early evening. The sun was out and the city glowed with the kind of light that is only created by the reflection of the sun on the sea. The place looked utterly beautiful. We stopped by at Rick's and picked up the post and I stayed in the van, as I couldn't bear the thought of seeing the door to our old flat. Boy, my spirits were low.

As we drove down to the seafront to park up for the night, I felt overwhelmed and homesick, and I felt silly as I realised I had tears streaming down my face.

"What is it?" Josh asked.

"I don't know," I whimpered. "I just feel really homesick."

"You'll feel better after a good night's sleep and a bit of sunshine."

He sounded tired, like he couldn't deal with this, and I knew he shouldn't have to. We had been having the best time ever and now I was crying because the weather had got me down. We both went straight to bed with a sombre mood hanging over us.

"How's it going, darling?" A familiar voice was at the other end of my mobile phone, waking me out of a deep slumber. It was my old friend Graham, who had recently moved to Peacehaven from London.

"Yeah, okay,"' I said, mid yawn and then, realising I had awoken feeling much better, I added, "Actually, I feel pretty good." In fact, the darkness inside me had passed and I felt great.

"Where are you now, then?"

"Brighton seafront." I laughed. "We've travelled far and wide."

"You be careful! Is that as far as you've got?"

I gave him a brief description of the journey so far and what we'd been up to.

"How does a nice hot bath and a double bed for the night sound to you all?"

"Fantastic! We'll cook the curry."

"Done deal."

"Enough said. See you later!"

I was looking forward to spending time with Graham by the time we pulled up outside his bungalow in Peacehaven at the end of the day.

"Hello, hello, hello, do come in!" Graham flung his door open wide in his usual welcoming way, his big, warm heart on his sleeve and a look on his handsome face that says he knows and loves you. He hugged us warmly and we were ushered into his lovely home. Wherever Graham is, he makes it homely. If he's waiting in a bus shelter for more than half an hour, you can guarantee he will start putting curtains up at the windows and scatter cushions on the bench, or at least be planning to. His homes are always cosy, interesting and give you that sink down, relax and rest kind of feeling.

Leela went berserk with his dogs, Dotty and Snoopy, both cheeky Jack Russells, and Dusty, a kind and beautiful Staffordshire bull terrier with sad, watery eyes. Marco, Graham's flatmate and an old friend from the heady Brixton days, was also home and we settled in for a feast and a proper catch-up.

As the evening wore on, I grew increasingly more tearful. I stopped drinking wine as I started to feel insecure about where my mood was heading and put on a brave face. Everyone noticed how quiet I had gone and kept asking if I was okay. It was all I could do to nod and smile weakly.

When Graham offered to run me a bath, I jumped at the chance to be on my own for a while. I sank gratefully into the bubbles and felt my body relax. The lyrics from a Guy Clark song wandered into my head:

Old friends, they shine like diamonds.
Old friends, you can always call.
Old friends, Lord, you can't buy 'em
Coz it's old friends after all.

I lay there for a long time and sobbed my heart out. I didn't care why and didn't have the energy to even try and make sense of it. It just felt good to let it all out.

At bedtime, Josh was very quiet. I knew he was confused by my behaviour and annoyed with me. We turned off the lights without saying goodnight. I pulled Leela into bed beside me and snuggled up to her. She was curled up in a foetal position, paws and nose tucked against my belly and chest, and it made me cry again.

Chapter Thirty-Four

Dreams come true

My eyes flew open in the middle of the night.

"I'm pregnant!" I told myself.

"No, you're not," said my sensible voice. "You're homesick and tired, get real."

"I'm four days late!"

"Don't be ridiculous, you were six months late last month, how can you just go back to a normal cycle?"

"Why do I feel sick then?"

"You don't."

"I did yesterday"

"No, you didn't, it was the smell in the van and the weather, and if you were pregnant, you would be feeling sick right now."

"I do a bit, I'm sure I do, only a bit, but I do feel sick."

"No, stop it, I'm not doing this again. You'll convince yourself, get all worked up, do a test and... Well, you know the rest."

The thought that I could be pregnant had popped into my head several times over the last few days, and I had shoved it away immediately, determined not to build up my hopes until I could be absolutely sure, and

I had to wait until I was at least a few days late before I could take a test result as the gospel truth. In the dead of night, my conscious mind wasn't quick enough to wipe away the words I so wanted to be true, and those words had turned into an argument before I could annihilate them. Now, there was no denying that being pregnant was a possibility.

I closed my eyes and willed myself back to sleep. No chance! I woke Josh up with the words, "I'm four days late now."

After a long pause, Josh suggested that we do a test once we were settled in a campsite. He was as reluctant as I was to have to experience another test that turned out to be negative.

"Just see how things go," he said. "Best not be too hasty. If you are, you are, and time will tell."

I was disappointed to find that I ate two lots of cereal and toast for breakfast and managed to keep it all down quite happily.

We looked up a few campsites on the internet and decided to head for one in the Ashdown forest. It was a sunny morning and the promise of a red-hot afternoon was in the air, so we cleaned and dried out the van and then headed into town for a few provisions and a pregnancy test.

We arrived at the campsite early afternoon. It was simple and lovely, with a fishing lake in the middle and plenty of room to find our own pitch. We opted for a place amongst the trees with the lake in view and then pegged ourselves out in the sun for the afternoon. It was heavenly seeing blue sky and feeling the sun warming our skin. I felt so much better – and so much worse because I felt so much better! Maybe it was the weather that had turned me, after all. We decided to do the pregnancy test the next morning.

I woke up early and got straight out of bed, fully intent on getting it over and done with as quickly as possible. I couldn't face the thought of doing it in a public loo with the possibility of someone waiting outside, so I found an empty hummus pot and peed in that. I felt sick to the bone as I unwrapped the stick and placed it in the pot. I counted to ten, just like the instructions said, pulled out the stick and put the cap on. Now, I had to wait two whole minutes for the result.

Josh was lying in bed and I knew he was pretending to be asleep, probably bracing himself for the moment I silently crawled back into bed and pulled the covers over my head for a cry, which had happened so many times before. I looked at the second hand on his watch and found that only forty seconds had gone by. There was another minute and twenty seconds to go! My throat was dry. If this test was negative, then I would have to accept that my hormones were up the swanny and I was most likely going through the menopause.

One minute left. I looked at the second hand. It appeared to be going backwards, then it went blurred. I snatched up the stick and stared at the blue vertical line that had appeared on the window. NOT PREGNANT. I felt faint with disappointment. This was so painful. I continued staring at the window as its authoritative answer to my question stared back.

"Please God, please let this be positive, make it that only thirty seconds has passed," I whispered. Then the unbelievable happened. A thin line started to appear horizontally across the window. I had visualised this so often that I thought I was imagining it. I blinked hard and opened my eyes wide.

"Oh, my God," I whispered. "Josh!" He didn't move. "I think it says I'm pregnant!"

He sat bolt upright and shuffled to the bottom of the bed. I handed him the stick and he squinted at it, then he moved it towards the light and pulled it closer to his eyes.

"What do you see?" I demanded

"A cross," he said weakly. "I think it's a cross."

We looked at each other and then looked at the stick again.

"It's definitely a cross, isn't it?" I said

We looked at each other again. "I think we've done it, we've finally done it. Oh, my God, we've finally done it!!!""

We hugged each other. I was laughing and crying at the same time and Josh was speechless.

"I need the toilet," he said and, pulling his yoga trousers on hastily, he opened the van door and disappeared.

Leela went with him. I sat in stillness and I must have said 'thank you' a hundred times before Josh appeared with a sheepish look on his face.

"Guess what?" he said

"What?"

"I just wet myself! I knew I was doing it but I just couldn't stop it, I feel like I'm in a dream."

We both collapsed into laughter. This was amazing. We were going to be parents at last; the baby we had been asking for was finally inside me.

We drifted through the day in a dream. It all felt perfectly normal and totally unreal at the same time. We took Leela for a walk to a lily pond near by. It was a lovely walk through the fields and woods and the pond looked like it belonged in a fairy-tale, with clear water and lotus flowers on the surface sandwiched between huge lily pads. There was no one around so we stripped off and dived in. The water was cold and felt fantastic. It began to rain slightly, gently spraying our faces as we swam across the lake.

Leela did her usual thing of panicking, jumping in and scratching us in her flurry of movement. We could never work out whether she was trying to save us, or climb on us for safety. Eventually, she gave up and went back to the bank onto dry land and ran back and forth, fussing about our welfare. I felt so alive in the water. I felt the little soul inside me and we talked to it as we swam, telling it how much fun we would have swimming in rivers and lakes, in all the different places we would travel to. I was forty-four years old and pregnant with my first child! I felt so happy, so in love with Josh and so connected to all the magic life has to offer.

Once we pulled ourselves out of the water, we got dressed quickly. Leela ducked and dived around us, obviously relieved we had seen sense and got onto dry land. Then we glided back to the van, made dinner and spent the rest of the evening sitting outside, listening to some folk music that people were playing nearby. The sound of the fiddle and the flute added to our dreamlike state. At one point in the evening, all the kids insisted the adults stop playing music and come to watch a show they had been creating. It was lovely to think that we would have this experience now, being with other families, watching our child play with other children.

We went to bed feeling like the luckiest people alive. *Thank you, thank you, thank you. Thank you, God; thank you, our child; thank you, universe…*

We pulled Leela close to us and thanked her, too. We knew she was a big part of this. She had changed our lives in so many ways, how could she not have a played a part in bringing our child to us?

Thank you, thank you, thank you, life; thank you, fairies; thank you, trees… After fifteen minutes or so, we couldn't think of anything else to thank, so we snuggled up close and thanked each other.

Chapter Thirty-Five

LEELA'S 1ST BIRTHDAY PARTY!

I found it so hard to keep the news to myself. On several occasions, I grabbed my phone ready to blurt out our news to my mum, or started a text to send out to everyone we knew. We decided to make a trip to our families as soon as possible, as we felt that once we had told our nearest and dearest, we could shout it from the rooftops. We decided to go to my family first, then travel back down and make the announcement to Josh's family in Birmingham.

It was funny, but as soon as the pregnancy was confirmed by the test, I had that feeling of 'Of course!' Of course I knew this was going to happen. I always knew I would be a mum! There was never any doubt in my mind that this child was here to stay. I had no sense that we needed to leave it three months before we announced it. I trusted myself in a way that I had never experienced before. I knew the pregnancy was strong and all was well.

I didn't feel the need to go to a doctor or have any medical checks at that point. I went to the cranial osteopath and, in his non invasive way, he confirmed my feelings that the pregnancy was healthy and strong. That was all the reassurance I needed. Now, it was time to announce and celebrate!

On the way up to Manchester, I was racking my brains to find a way to get all my family together without them guessing we were finally going to make The Announcement that they had all hoped for at some point. Then I had the perfect idea and I prepared a text: *You are invited to Leela's 1st birthday party on Sunday, 7th September. Big curry will be made at the Tew residence and frivolities to be had. 4pm onwards. RSVP.*

I knew Kaye and Paul wouldn't mind me inviting them to their own home for a curry. That's the great thing about family; you are always at home, no matter whose home you are in. Leela's birthday wasn't actually until the 9th, but we checked it with her and she was fine about celebrating early. I got replies from everyone within the hour, including all the nephews and nieces. They were all up for it.

"They're all mad. Do they realise they are coming to a dog's birthday party?" Josh said.

"They probably feel sorry for us and think it's too sensitive a subject to take the mickey!" I laughed.

I could imagine each family member receiving the text and rolling their eyes and then figuring all they could do was humour us as, after all, the chances of them getting invited to our child's birthday party were looking pretty slim.

We enjoyed planning how we would make our announcement. It was now Saturday and I thought I would burst with the news way before Sunday afternoon. How on earth could I keep this from them? Surely they would take one look at my greenish complexion and out-of-place grin and put two and two together? The thought of watching them all gathering for Leela's birthday kept me going.

"We'll have to play it really seriously, be excited about it and look hurt if anyone makes a joke," I instructed Josh.

"We'll make them sing *Happy Birthday* to her," he said

"And hint at presents," I enthused

"No, maybe that's a step too far. We'll lose credibility," said Josh.

In the end, we decided to play it cool with the presents but take the celebration really seriously. It would be jolly good sport for a Sunday afternoon!

We stayed over at Mum's on the Saturday night. I feigned a cold and went to bed early after picking at my dinner. Mum didn't

seem overly concerned or suspicious of anything, so we had overcome the first hurdle. Next day, Josh went shopping for the ingredients for the feast.

"Please don't ask me to help you with anything to do with food. I'm not even sure I'll be able to stay in the kitchen," I warned Josh.

We got to Kaye and Paul's about midday and Josh started cooking. I was doing my best to hide the fact that I felt like poo, but when the smell of onion, garlic and spices started to fill the house, I had to get out. I suggested we walked the dogs. I was avoiding having any eye contact with my sisters or my mum for fear of blurting it out, but if I was in a crowd I could just about contain myself. I managed to get my sisters and two of my nieces to come with us by using the fact that Leela would love as many people as possible to join her in her birthday walk. I think this irritated everybody somewhat, but they came along all the same.

The fresh air did me the world of good. I fell into step with my niece Bethany as we walked along the river. The previous year, Beth and I had spent a whole afternoon creating my dreams on a computer game called *The Simms*. We had been talking about the law of attraction and how much I wanted a baby and she had suggested we create it on her computer game. We had built our dream home on a piece of land shared by other families and created two children for us, a boy and a girl. Beth had been twelve then and was so excited at the thought of having another cousin. I had been really touched, watching her get so involved, taking every detail seriously, creating the beautiful countryside we would live in and trying to make the people look like us as much as she could. As I walked beside her now, I was itching to tell her that part of that dream was about to come true!

When we got back to the house, my nausea had passed and I felt more able to join in the party mood. People came a bit early for a drink and we all stayed in the kitchen-diner. Josh was enjoying doing what he does best, cooking. He had taken the part of party girl's dad very seriously and had thrown himself into the role. He kept calling Leela over and making a fuss, singing *Happy Birthday*, asking what she would like on the menu. I kept trying to catch his eye to calm him down a bit. He was way over the top and someone was going to get suspicious. When he went so far as to pick Leela up and ask her how she would like the place settings,

I just had to pull him to one side and have a word. He looked surprised as I broke the news that his acting stunk, but he got my point!

Dinner was ready by four and everyone had arrived – sisters with their husbands and children, and Mum and Joe. We poured the champagne and put the party hat on Leela, picked her up and everybody sang *Happy Birthday* to her. It was hilarious! I looked round at my daft family singing to my dog, clutching their glasses of champagne and smiling away and loved them so much, yet, at the same time I felt slightly fearful that this was my family and they were smiling away, clutching their champagne and singing to my dog! Song over, we all cheered and clinked glasses, then they sat down to eat.

Josh and I stood at the end of the table. Leela had wriggled out of his arms and run off into the garden with her hat swinging round her neck by the elastic, no doubt thankful her bit was over and she could stop pretending now. Josh and I looked at each other.

"Go on," he said.

"You do it." I was suddenly lost for words.

"No, you do it. Quick, you'll lose the moment."

I panicked, as everyone's attention had turned to food. If they got their mitts on those poppadoms now, we'd never get them back "Oh, hang on! Just one more toast for Tuesday, which is actually her birthday," I spluttered. That did it. They all looked up, a little concerned for my mental health. I seized the moment.

"Actually, the real reason you are here is that we are going to have a baby."

Complete silence. My whole family turned to stone. It was the quietest moment in the Campbell family history. My thoughts went crazy during the next half a second: *Oh no, they look angry. No, they think I'm joking. They're going to have a mass heart attack! No, they don't understand, they think Leela's pregnant!*

"We are pregnant! *I'm* pregnant!" I said, mimicking a crazed foreigner shouting louder and louder and emphasising each word as I mimed a big belly.

Another unanimous intake of breath and then all the females burst into tears. It was complete chaos – tears, congratulations, kisses and hugs and everyone talking at once. Mum was hysterical with happiness. Hannah, Bethany and Lauren were covered in mascara and Maxine and Molly were hugging all the dogs and telling them the news. Kaye nearly passed out, then got a migraine and had to go and lie down and all the men looked slightly bewildered. Family life had returned to normal.

EPILOGUE

It's now February 2015 and I am sitting in our kitchen, watching Anousha play in our beautiful garden with her friends. It is by no means the end of my journey, but it's a pretty good place to say *au revoir*. Life is good. It feels rich and deep and satisfying and I feel a sense of peace and contentment with who I am.

I had a fabulous pregnancy. I decided very early on that I didn't want to go down the medical route unless it was necessary. It was fantastic timing that donna Eden's book *Energy Medicine for Women* came out in the early weeks containing all the exercises I needed to end the morning sickness and stay vibrant and strong. I chose not to have any scans and, instead, to trust mine and Josh's instinct, along with the support of Jonathan and Sarah. If I'd gone the normal medical route, I knew I would be put in a 'high risk bracket' due to my age and therefore be kept on close watch. I also knew that being on close watch and being presented with the worst-case scenario at each scan would make me anxious and I felt the most important factor in a healthy pregnancy was to be stress-free.

Not much attention gets paid to how much stress and worry affect us on a physical level and, after reading *The Secret Life of the Unborn Child*, by Dr Thomas

Verny with John Kelly, and watching *Nature, Nurture and the Power of Love* by Bruce Lipton, I understood that my attitude and emotional state were very important to this little being that was growing inside me. Babies are aware of their mother's feelings and experiences from very early on in the womb, some believe from the moment of conception. Throughout my pregnancy, my attitude to life was shaping the baby's; its decisions on whether the world was full of friends or foes, a safe place or a terrain full of dangers, a dull existence, or one full of wonder and beauty – all the qualities that were seen as important in a bygone time when women were in charge of pregnancy and birth, and experience was rated just as much as qualification.

My choices weren't a slight towards the medical profession. Had I been worried or needed any reassurance, I would not have hesitated in contacting my doctor. I have a deep respect for many of the things the medical profession has to offer and I know that it has saved many a woman and baby's life in pregnancy and birth and, on the whole, midwives and other health care professionals care deeply and do an incredible job. I also feel that the system is far too imposing, due to protocol and standard procedures, the magic has been stripped out of this sacred ritual of bringing life onto Earth. Like many other areas in our culture, pregnancy and birth has become a business to be managed and controlled. I didn't want this miracle I was experiencing to be turned into diary full of appointments, where I was weighed, measured, prodded and poked. I also believe that scans are invasive to the baby and should be offered only if deemed necessary, not as routine or for curiosity. I wanted to be left to experience the initiation of becoming a mother without worry or waiting for the next appointment to reassure me; to enjoy having another soul growing inside me, knowing my job was to nurture myself and maintain a sense of wonder and respect for life. Having said that, I think everybody should have the right to take the route that is best for them; there are many people in this world and therefore many different opinions and ways of doing things. There is no 'right way'. I would encourage anyone to follow their heart and take time to feel what is right for them in any situation. Experts have their place and knowledge and wisdom should be passed on, but I believe instinct should also be valued and encouraged in our decision-making.

After researching natural birth, we found a wonderful doula to support us. A doula is someone who offers emotional and practical support to a woman (or couple) before, during and after childbirth.

I feel really blessed to have had Samsara with me. The moment we met her, we knew she was the woman we wanted to support us through this intimate journey. She was kind, warm, supportive and empowering. Samsara had a gentle and firm way of holding us without propping us up, and, her vast experience of birth and obvious love and respect for the miracle of a woman's body gave me every confidence that I could do it! She also prepared me for the fact that sometimes, medical intervention is needed. So I left my hospital bag packed and out of sight in case of an emergency, and focused on having a home birth.

Josh, Leela and I had a wonderful time in those months of preparation. We moved out of the van in the depths of winter and stayed with our good friend Alex in Brighton for a month, before we found a house to rent in Ringmer, a beautiful little cottage aptly named White Cottage, with a huge garden next to open fields. Josh and I were stepping into the unknown together, both incredibly excited and full of the wonder of life and all that it had brought us in the last year. We fell in love all over again, laughed until we thought our sides would split at comedy films, walked Leela through endless breathtaking countryside and enjoyed our roaring open fire as winter raged outside.

In the last few months, as winter turned into spring, we hired a birthing pool and enjoyed evenings splashing about in the water and relieving me of my enormous bulk! When I was thirty-five weeks, we went to a midwife and finally registered ourselves as pregnant. I always booked an appointment with Jonathan after my bi-weekly appointment with the midwife and, it was interesting that he would give me exactly the same information that the midwife had just given us about the position of the baby and how close it was to being ready, etc., simply by placing his hands on my lower back, or my feet and sensing what was going on in my body.

I had a long labour and the baby was not in the optimal position for birth. We were back to back, which made it very painful. Josh, Leela and Samsara never left my side and I went through seven midwives as they came and went with their shifts. Although each midwife was caring and attentive, it was difficult for me when they, quite understandably, had to leave at the end of their shift and I was so glad we had chosen to have a doula, as Samsara was a constant source of support for both of us.

Labour was a wonderful mix of dipping in and out of other worlds, feeling connected to Josh, then completely alone and afraid, feeling pain and pleasure and total exhaustion. By Tuesday afternoon, it was established that the baby's head was twisted and wasn't bearing down on my cervix so I wasn't dilating, and by Tuesday early evening I had stopped labouring and I was exhausted and semi delirious from three nights of no sleep.

At that point, it was clear that I needed medical support. We all sat in the living room of the cottage and waited for the ambulance, which we were informed would be arriving in ten minutes. I began to feel scared that things weren't going to plan and I was also worried about leaving Leela. She knew something was wrong and we were about to leave her alone, which would be distressing for her, to say the least. It was too late to find someone to be with her and I began to feel panicky, as this was a part of the story I couldn't relate to or understand.

As my tension was rising, there was a knock on the door and, thinking it was the ambulance, Josh went to open it. I heard the voice of our friend Chris and a feeling of relief flooded through me. Chris was on his way to see his mother, who lived close by and often looked after Leela when we needed it. As all our friends knew that our baby was thirteen days overdue and, that we were planning a home birth, no one was 'popping in', but Chris said that for some reason, as he was passing, he knew he had to come and knock on the door.

After a brief explanation, Leela was out the door, her midwifery shift over, waggling her tail like crazy as she jumped in Chris's car, ready for a well-deserved break.

For Josh and I, it was a massive relief and a sign that all was heading in the right direction. My fear of going to hospital dissipated. I knew we were being supported and all would be well.

At the hospital, Josh handed the midwife our birth plan that stated all my wishes for my birth, should I end up in hospital. Amongst a few other requests, I wanted the minimal amount of intervention and total silence at the time of birth. This was totally respected. After a discussion with the obstetrician who was concerned at how long I had been in labour, I agreed to have an epidural as the pain was making me vomit what little I had left inside me and I desperately needed to rest. It was such a relief to lie down, pain-free and sleep. Josh and Samsara slept on the floor. The plan was that the epidural would allow me to sleep and let synthetic oxytocin do its job so, in the morning, I would have the strength to give birth.

This was not what I had wanted. I had read so much about how synthetic oxytocin and epidurals can prevent the natural bonding that was so essential at birth. At this point, though, I was too tired to cling onto my ideal scenario of how our baby would be born. I honestly think that for me, this was the time that I stopped being a pregnant woman and became a mother. I didn't care about my ideals any more. I wanted my baby to be safe and I wanted to deliver it safely into this world and I was no longer in a position to do that without medical support. This is not to say that I was willing to just hand everything over to the medical team and that my body no longer mattered. I still wanted a say in what was happening, but I knew it was important to accept and make plan B, plan A.

In the night, I was monitored and when the baby showed signs of distress, Josh strengthened my heart meridian by holding certain points on my body and the baby stabilised. In the morning, the contractions started to come thick and fast. The epidural had worn off a fair bit and I could feel a little again. A mix of four nights of very little sleep and the drugs had put me in a strange and altered state. Josh was by my side and I finally managed to muster up my last bit of strength and was pushing hard with my eyes tightly shut when I heard Samsara's voice whisper in my ear, "Look at your baby."

I opened my eyes to see our beautiful baby being held above me. Then the cord was cut and she was whisked away to be checked, which I felt was an unnecessary part of the protocol and the part of the birth I found the most difficult to accept. However it was only seconds before Josh brought her back to me and, as he handed me our child, he said, "It's a little girl." I held her tiny body close to my breast and Josh sat beside me, speechless. Samsara slipped quietly away and Josh and I were left alone together to have our first family moments.

I have no words to describe how I felt just then; only the word 'massive' comes to mind. Massive amounts of love, joy, bewilderment and more love and joy. Life would never be the same again. I was a mother at last, and Josh was a father. After a while, she opened her little mouth and breastfed for the first time and I felt I could move a mountain.

When she had finished feeding, Josh held her and we stared some more. Then he handed her back and we smiled at each other again and stared at her some more. This little, wrinkled, beige beauty that I had felt growing inside me for the last few months, was now in my arms. Perfect, tiny little fingers wrapped around mine. I gazed at her little screwed-up face, every inch of her a miracle. Who can ever describe that moment you meet your child? Time stood still and nothing else mattered. I breathed in that heavenly new born smell and stroked her soft plump cheek, her lips puckered and she let out a tiny sound that sent a wave of joy through the whole of my being. Outside the window was a view of rolling hills; a beautiful, misty, warm spring morning had dawned. A view that eventually led us to call her Anousha, meaning a beautiful morning.

We were home by that evening and when Leela returned, she quickly sniffed her little sister and, instead of waiting to be invited to sit next to me on the bed like she always did, she assumed a position next to us on the floor. She slotted into her new role easily, seeming to understand that there was a new and vulnerable member in our pack. I, on the other hand, went through what most mothers have since told me that they experienced with their second child. In those heady days of being a new mum, I also mourned my old relationship with Leela as she formed a stronger bond with Josh and we no longer had our one-on-one time together. In a way, it was a relief, as so many people had told me I would not have the same feeling towards Leela once the baby came. I was happy and relieved to know I loved her just as much as before.

It felt totally natural becoming a mum. Despite my fear of the nature of her birth interfering with the bonding process, I didn't have any problems in feeling deeply connected to her from day one. It felt right and easy to follow Anousha's guidance and respond to her cues and rhythms, rather than try and train her into a routine that was governed by the clock. She stayed in my sling and I got on with life as normal. I took her with me wherever I went and always assumed she was welcome. She slept with us and fed on demand. I got plenty of sleep because she was content and easily had her needs met. She would wake regularly for feeds and often help herself whilst I stayed in a light sleep. Samsara had introduced me to a great book, *Three In a Bed* by Deborah Jackson, whilst I was pregnant and I think the advice made a huge contribution to making life with a new born easy and joyful. There are many fears and warnings that lead people to believe that sleeping with their baby is unsafe, and, although some are valid (I would recommend anybody to do some research if they are considering co-sleeping to be sure that they don't fit into the exceptions) – on the whole, research has shown that it is a natural and safe way to care for your infant in the wee hours.

We continued to enjoy a good social life whilst she got to know the world from the safety of our sling, which either Josh or I wore so she was always close to us. I still attended workshops and talks and went to parties and gigs (with baby ear protectors at the ready!). When the retreat weekends started at Oxon Hoath, Anousha came along with us. Whilst I taught, Josh was with Anousha and vice versa and, on a few occasions she remained with us when we taught together.

I don't put everything down to the way we chose to do things – all babies have their different characters and adults have their different needs – but I do feel that being able to be fully present and relaxed, along with following the baby's rhythm and allowing them to be included in adult as well as baby activities, helps them develop a sense of belonging and contentment. I also acknowledge that we had the perfect circumstances in which to parent in exactly the way we wanted to and I feel incredibly grateful for that.

Our time of transitioning homes lasted another two years. We moved from White Cottage when Anousha was six months old and into a small house in Lewes. We stayed there for two years, which was long enough to make many new friends and fall in love with this quirky town that offers lots of alternative culture and masses of character, along with a firm sense of community. In the heart of the town, The Phoenix industrial estate is a treasure to be discovered. Inside the run-down buildings that are rented out by artists, performers and social activists, beautiful spaces have been created offering great venues for music, talks, workshops and community gatherings. We realised that we had found the community we had been visioning for a long time and were intent on staying.

When we were told that our little house was going up for sale, we started looking for alternative accommodation in Lewes. One day, Josh was on his way to the train station and, on the off-chance, he popped into the estate agent's office to speak to Chris, the agent who had found us White Cottage.

As soon as Chris saw Josh, he held up some specs for a property that had just come in and said, "I have your dream home." He gave Josh the details of an annexe that was attached to a cottage in Laughton.

When he brought them home, my first response was, "No way!" I was in love with Lewes and blown away by what we had found there. Laughton was six miles away and out in the sticks. However, Josh was up for giving it a chance and he reminded me of how fixed we had become about Brighton and that we had promised ourselves not to cling on too hard to anything, after all the magic we had experienced by going with the flow. So I sat with the details for a while.

The place certainly looked amazing; it was just in the wrong place! Even so, after my initial reaction faded, I decided to give it a chance and at least go and view it. We went on a dismal February morning when everything looked bleak and dull, but it was still beautiful. It was an annexe, with a huge lounge that used to be a games room for the landlord and landlady's six children, and two decent-sized bedrooms that each had French doors opening up into a private garden, which led to a shared orchard. At the end of the orchard, across a quiet road, were miles and miles of woodland. We went back to Lewes knowing we had to give it a go.

I was still a little apprehensive and, that evening, while I was chatting to Marlene on the phone, I mentioned it and she did a quick dowse for us and got a huge positive on us moving there. Although we had already decided to move it was great to get confirmation and gave room to let go of the slight doubt and get fully excited. I can't remember a time when Marlene's dowsing turned out to be wrong; this time was no exception.

I certainly wouldn't have consciously chosen to live here, as, heavenly as it is, I always saw myself as a hustle and bustle kind of a person, needing people around me and plenty of options for entertainment available. Yet here in Laughton, I find I am happier and more grounded and content than I have ever been; and Lewes is still a big part of our lives.

Being a mum has given me the chance to reflect and put into practice all the values I had before I was a parent. My beliefs that human beings are innately joyful, sociable, co-operative and kind, and that control and authoritarian approaches leave us to doubt and push against our true nature and each other, have been strengthened.

I have also come up against my own habits and conditionings that are a far cry from the compassionate and trusting person I want to be. It has been the best ongoing, most advanced self-development course I could ever imagine; life at its rawest, most passionate and real. Anousha is a contented person, but by no means a pushover. She is fiercely independent and has a determination that I am in awe of, even though it has tested me to my limits, as I struggled against my own conditioning to control her at times when it would have been easier to do so for a quick and short-term solution. However, I believe and have experienced it enough to know that a good leader is listened to because they make sense, not because they demand obedience and that, in the long run, respect and kindness create a relationship of trust and ease.

I remember watching Anousha dance when she was around two years old and thinking, *she is doing this for her own pleasure*. In fact, she does everything for the experience of pleasure. She draws, dances, learns to walk and talk, all because it feels good, because life is a pleasure – a pleasure that naturally serves her impulse to evolve.

Our job as parents is to keep that intact. I want her to do everything in life because it feels good and fulfilling, not because she gets a certificate for it, or a round of applause, or praise from someone. I want to share her joy and passions without judging that she is 'good' or she's 'done well', or putting a grade on it. I want her to be the judge of how well she does and that judgement will come from her inner feeling of how good it feels, how fulfilling it is, not how happy she has made everybody else, or how much she has been approved of.

I believe self-directed people are truly happy, and happy people are naturally generous and kind, the type of people our culture needs right now. We don't need to teach children these things, we simply need to model it ourselves, so they can stay in touch with what is natural to them. Children learn what they live. I don't believe we come into this world looking for approval; we come in fully expecting to be nurtured and cared for and loved purely because we exist. I find it interesting how quick people are to judge a child when they don't comply, when they do have a mind of their own and are not easily manipulated. It isn't comfortable for us. And yet ask any parent about the qualities they would like to see in their children as adults and, most would want the very qualities that we deem inappropriate for them as children.

Children are rarely awarded the same rights or respect as adults. They are often talked about as if they are not there, told how to behave and what to say, judged and commented on in ways we deem are rude if they ever do the same to us. Too often, we tell them to do one thing, and then model the opposite. The founder of NVC (Non Violent Communication) starts one of his workshops by asking the participants how they would deal with a situation whereby a neighbour has borrowed something precious and not returned it. The group is then split into two and, without realising that each group has been given different instructions, one group is told they are dealing with a child and another with an adult. Always, when the group come together again and put their heads together to discuss their solutions, it is plain that the group who were dealing with the adult show far more respect and kindness than the group dealing with the child.

We learn through observation and imitation, and kindness and respect beget kindness and respect. If we want our children to be respectful, co-operative, reasonable and respectable, it makes sense that we treat them with such virtues. Our long-held cultural belief that children need to be moulded and told how to behave in order to fit into society and coerced into achieving and becoming something, is a myth that needs to be discarded if we are to find peace and happiness again in our world of endless possibilities.

The more Josh and I trust Anousha and leave her to make her own decisions, the more I see that she naturally veers towards making healthy choices for herself, and she is also more willing to listen to us if we offer some advice or another point of view. Sure, she has her days when she indulges and she sometimes gets overtired just like we all do, but on the whole, without us having to lay any rules down, she balances her diet well and gets plenty of rest when she needs it. I don't want an obedient child, I want her to listen to me because she trusts me as a partner in her life; because I have something of value to offer her, not because she is afraid I will be angry or that I will withdraw my love if she 'disobeys'. Nor do I want her to do things to earn my praise or to try and please me. You can't force someone to respect you; they either do or they don't and obedience and respect are a far cry from each other; as are compliance and co-operation.

I feel that our society has become far too institutionalized and there is less and less freedom to choose, as the options narrow down and we are all herded along the same path, fed the same education and led into careers according to our ability. Although there are many amazing teachers out there who are making a positive impact, our systems are not set up to allow people to be free to reach their full potential. We are conditioned to live for the future, rather than enjoy the present. Now that I am a parent, it is more apparent than ever that our culture lives in a context where schooling is valued over family, routine over spontaneity, and achievement over happiness. And yet, I see in children that the opposite is true for them. We are conditioned into these values. In our hearts, I believe every human being would choose joy, freedom, connection and co-operation if trusted to do so. It's our natural way of being.

These beliefs have led Josh and I to choose the un-schooling route as regards to education. We follow our own rhythms as much as possible, our curriculum is born out of our passions and interests. Along with a group of other families, we use the world as our classroom and the three R's crop up naturally in everyday life. Watching the children learn without any formal teaching is fascinating. Their interest and passion to know more about their world is their motivation.

They don't need to be tested or measured; if anything, that kills off their willingness to be happy participants in our society. I believe children need to be cared for, and our role as adults is to do that by supporting their passions. As children, they have their limitations, but their right to be respected and trusted and left to form their own views as people in their own right, should be equal to any adult's.

Life is good now and I know it is good because of my commitment to feeling good from the inside. Years of embracing and transforming the parts of myself that I have disliked, even hated and most certainly rejected in the past, along with cultivating a sense of peace and contentment with life has paid off. My happiness isn't because of the baby, the husband, the house, the dog or the way of life, although they certainly help and I am incredibly grateful for what I have. Living is still a process with its up and downs, but I feel more and more in touch with my true nature, a nature that wants to be wild and free. Incidentally, my view of what it is to be wild has changed dramatically since my twenties! Nowadays, my wild side wants me to be intrinsically motivated, in touch with nature and the needs of my body. It wants to me to dance like nobody's watching and sing because I love to sing. She wants me to live authentically and respect diversity. Co-operate and be kind and generous, but never to the detriment of my own needs. She wants me to be truly happy and free by being at peace with who I am, with a deep knowing that I am enough.

This is what I aspire to regain for myself and protect in my daughter, because she already lives these qualities, as every child is born with them.

And of course, there is always Leela, reminding us to let life live us...

Authors note.

A huge thank you to everyone who helped me get the book to this stage. Special thanks to my editor Lorna Read, also for all your suggestions and support, Kaye Tew for editing early drafts and encouraging me to get the story written in the first place. Judith Antell, Kaye Tew, Roma Hearsey, Alice Field and Nicky Aisher for the read throughs comments and final amendments. Josh for your love and support and Anousha and Leela for your inspiration.

If you would like to stay in touch please visit me at:

www.liannecampbell.com

Lightning Source UK Ltd.
Milton Keynes UK
UKHW01f0612310518
323512UK00001B/172/P

9 781781 489086